A to Z

Practical learning strategies
to support **Spiritual** and **Moral Development**

Joyce Mackley and **Pamela Draycott**

REtoday
Services

RE Today Services, a part of Christian Education, is an ecumenical educational charity which works throughout the United Kingdom.

Its aims are:

- to support Religious Education in schools;
- to increase awareness of the spiritual, moral, social and cultural dimensions of the curriculum;
- to articulate Christian perspectives on education.

RE Today Services is committed to the teaching of the major world faiths in Religious Education, and to an accurate and fair representation of their beliefs, values and practices in all its teaching materials.

RE Today Services fulfils these aims:

- by publishing teaching materials like this book and background papers together with a termly magazine *REtoday*, and distributing the *British Journal of Religious Education*;
- by offering professional development and consultancy services through its professional staff;
- by arranging national and regional courses for teachers, pupils and others interested in education;
- by research and curriculum development work;
- by supporting the Professional Council for Religious Education and distributing its journal *Resource*.

The first edition of the *A to Z Active Learning Strategies* developed out of a Templeton Foundation and CEM (now RE Today Services) project entitled 'Looking Inwards Looking Outwards'. This second fully revised, updated and expanded edition takes account of recent educational initiatives and builds on that work, drawing on the developmental work of the RE Today Professional Services team.

By Joyce Mackley and Pamela Draycott

Illustrated by Phil Vernon

Thanks to Holy Trinity CofE Primary School, Cheltenham, Holte School, Birmingham, and St Andrew's Primary School, JHQ, Germany, for permission to reproduce photographs on the front cover and in the 'Pictures and Photographs' section..

Published by Christian Education Publications
1020 Bristol Road
Selly Oak
Birmingham
B29 6LB

British Cataloguing-in-Publication data
A catalogue record for this book is available from the British Library.

ISBN 1-904024-55-6

First published 2004

Designed and typeset by Christian Education Publications

Printed and bound by Herald Forms Group

Introduction

This *A to Z* provides busy teachers with a range of stimulus ideas for practical learning strategies to use in their teaching. It is not designed to give fully worked out lesson outlines or to provide all the answers in encouraging active participation. Rather it is offered as a stimulus for ideas, thought and action.

The introductory section addresses some issues surrounding active learning and spiritual and moral development within the context of Religious Education. It does however have wider application to other areas of the curriculum such as, for example, Personal, Health and Social Education (PHSE) or English. It is also applicable to the whole area of Citizenship. Many of the learning strategies suggested are suitable across the age and ability ranges. Teachers will need to use their knowledge of the pupils and their own professional judgement in order to select, adapt and develop relevant activities.

Joyce Mackley and Pamela Draycott

The *A to Z* is offered as a stimulus for ideas, thought and action

Contents

Introduction 3

Setting the scene – some educational issues 4

A to Z practical learning strategies 15

Index of strategies 78

Index of RE topics 79

Some useful resources 80

I hear, I forget
I see, I remember
I do, I understand

Setting the scene – some educational issues

Personal development, particularly in relation to the spiritual, moral, social and cultural development of pupils and students is a key element of education. Inspection emphasis rightly links these aspects of personal development with academic achievement and with the raising of standards of attainment.

Five propositions

The purpose of education is to foster personal growth

- The purpose of education is to foster personal growth (academically, physically, spiritually, morally, socially and culturally) in order to help realise human potential.
- The whole curriculum should support this aim.
- Spiritual and moral development is central to this aim, and should pervade the whole curriculum.
- Religious Education (RE) has a particular role to play within spiritual and moral development.
- In promoting personal growth and development, the processes of education are as important as the content.

Spiritual and moral development

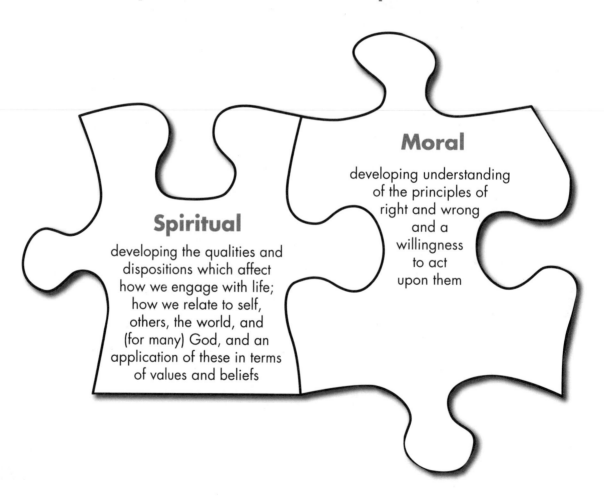

Spiritual

developing the qualities and dispositions which affect how we engage with life; how we relate to self, others, the world, and (for many) God, and an application of these in terms of values and beliefs

Moral

developing understanding of the principles of right and wrong and a willingness to act upon them

REtoday
Services

AtoZ

A model for quality RE

Shared human experience

Those experiences common to all human beings which raise questions of meaning and purpose

Learning about...
Learning from...

RE

Living belief systems

For example, Christianity, Buddhism, Hinduism, Islam, Judaism, Sikhism

Learning about...
Learning from...

Personal search

Who am I?
Does my life have any significance?
Where did I come from?
Where am I going?

Learning about...
Learning from...

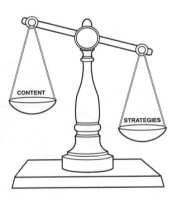

This model provides a framework for considering what RE is and how it relates to human experience and personal development.

- **Shared human experience** concerns such questions as 'What does it mean to be human?'
- **Personal search** considers 'What does it mean to be me?'
- **Living belief systems** brings these two dimensions together by drawing on the insights and answers offered, and the further questions raised, by religious and non-religious beliefs today.

Good RE is a balance between learning *about* the teachings and insights of world faiths and enabling pupils to *draw meaning* for their own lives *from* this learning. Traditional teaching methods can give pupils knowledge and understanding about religions, but engaging pupils in reflection, application and expression of these ideas and teachings requires a different approach.

Getting pupils involved

Activities, tasks and strategies most likely to promote engagement and develop pupils' spiritual and moral development will make sure that pupils:

- **reprocess not regurgitate** – that they work with ideas, beliefs, values and practices. They reflect on them, apply them, respond to them and evaluate them.
- **use both right and left brain functions** – that learning activities ensure a balance between logic, order, analysis and creativity and self-expression.
- **use all the senses** – touch, taste, smell, sight, hearing.
- **engage both heart and mind** – effective learning 'touches the person'.
- **are actively involved** – we remember best that which we do for ourselves.
- **build on the strengths and abilities** they have.
- **enjoy what they do** – have fun.

The teaching and learning process

Good Religious Education engages learners in a process whereby they pursue their personal questions about meaning and purpose in the context of questions raised by human experience, drawing on the insights offered by major world faiths. This process has four main interrelated aspects – engaging, exploring, expressing and responding.

Engaging It is good practice to start with the familiar and widen into the new and unfamiliar. The starting point for spiritual and moral development is human experience.

Exploring Move on into an exploration and reflection on the deeper questions and issues this raises. Such exploration is not primarily 'book-based' but developed through activities such as:

- **experiential and reflective activities** such as stilling, relaxation and visualisation;
- **engaging the senses** – sight, sound, touch, taste and smell;
- **expressive arts** – art, poetry, music, drama and dance engage pupils' imaginative and creative capacities.

Expressing Use carefully designed active strategies which enable pupils to express their own insights and responses. This may or may not use words. It can be creative and use expressive arts such as painting, poetry, music, dance and drama.

Responding Response is the developing recognition, over time, of personal beliefs, values and attitudes. Enable pupils to reflect on the implications of their learning for their own action and attitudes. Ensure opportunities for taking responsible action in light of their learning.

Good RE enables learners to pursue personal questions in the context of human experience, drawing on insights offered by world faiths

1 Engaging
with real-life situations, stories, opinions and teachings which raise questions of meaning and purpose

2 Exploring
the issues and reflecting on them in relation to the insights of world faiths by a variety of active learning methods

3 Expressing
our own reactions to these experiences and insights in a variety of ways, including artistic forms of expression

4 Responding
in active ways, including increasing recognition of our own beliefs and values and significant changes in behaviour

REtoday Services

AtoZ

Learning styles

We are all different. We learn differently.

If we want all pupils to be able to participate fully in their learning we need to plan to ensure a wide range of learning styles is provided for.

Three common models are:

- **sensory preferences** – Bandler and Grinder's theory that everyone has a dominant sense – their visual, auditory or kinaesthetic sense (VAK).

- **cognitive preferences –** Anthony Gregorc's analysis of how information is perceived and ordered.

- **intelligence profiles** – Howard Gardner's theory of multiple intelligences or 'frames of mind'.

Implications for teaching

Whichever model is adopted, **teachers need** to be aware:

- of their own preferred learning style, and ensure that this does not dominate in their classroom;

- of the preferred learning styles of their pupils, but avoid 'pigeonholing';

- that preferred learning styles may change with time;

- that people generally learn best in a variety of ways and one needs to plan a range of opportunities to allow them to do so.

> A learning style is...
> a preferred way of using one's abilities. It is not in itself an ability but rather a preference.
> *Robert Sternberg*

> 'Intelligence may be regarded as the capacity to learn. There is general agreement that intelligence is not a fixed commodity.'
> *Key Stage 3 Training Materials, 2002*

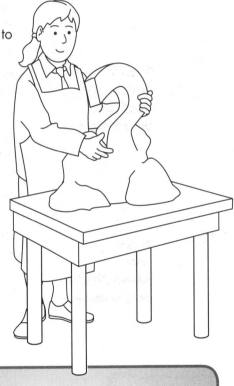

See also...

- ***The Teacher's Toolkit*** by Paul Ginnis (Crown House Publishing Limited, 2002, ISBN 1-899-83-676-4)

- ***Accelerated Learning in Practice*** by Alistair Smith (Network Educational Press Ltd, 2000, ISBN 1-855-39-048-5)

- ***From thinking skills to thinking classrooms*** by C McGuinness (DfEE Research Report RR115) – a review of approaches to developing pupils' thinking

VAK – visual, auditory, kinaesthetic preferences

We all have a dominant sense and this is our most efficient and preferred way of learning

Use of seeing (visual), hearing (audio) and doing (kinaesthetic) approaches to learning increases the chance of pupils engaging with their learning and connecting current work with previous learning and experience.

At the heart of the VAK approach is the conviction that we all have a dominant sense and that this is our most efficient and preferred way of learning. For much of the time the three senses work in conjunction, and in different combinations as required by different situations.

Research suggests that in any class in any school there are on average 29% of pupils with visual dominance, 34% with auditory and 37% with kinaesthetic dominance (*The Teacher's Toolkit,* Paul Ginnis, 2002, page 39).

What does this mean for the RE classroom?

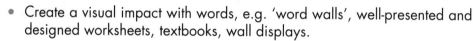
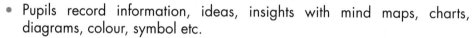

Some teaching strategies

Seeing
Pupils with visual preference

- Use visual stimulus activities, e.g. videos, posters, visits, OHP, *PowerPoint,* diagrams and charts, photographs, well-illustrated textbooks and activity sheets.
- Create a visual impact with words, e.g. 'word walls', well-presented and designed worksheets, textbooks, wall displays.
- Pupils record information, ideas, insights with mind maps, charts, diagrams, colour, symbol etc.

Hearing
Pupils with auditory preference

- Video-, audio- and ICT-based stimuli with interesting and varied commentary and soundtracks, e.g. religious sounds, extracts from speeches and interviews, audio novels, music, stories.
- Presentations with peers in a range of contexts.
- Pupils make audio tapes or use sound, e.g. percussion instruments to express meanings in stories etc.
- Discussion (paired, group or class) and feedback.
- Guest speakers.

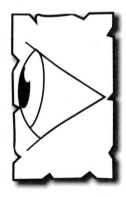

Doing
Pupils with kinaesthetic preference

- Learning opportunities which involve making, sorting, arranging, handling items such as religious artefacts (as appropriate).
- Opportunities for role-play; human barchart; freeze-frame, variety of discussion group formats; moving between resources; visits.

Characteristics of intelligence

Knowledge of workings of the brain has begun to impact on approaches to teaching and learning. Howard Gardner identified eight types of 'intelligence'. As Gardner has claimed, 'they rarely operate independently ... they complement each other as people develop skills or solve problems.' Many people have a 'natural' inclination towards one or two of these types, but most of us, given the right stimuli, are able to develop abilities in the other areas also.

In RE it is essential to recognise these different 'intelligences' when planning activities. Traditional methods have really only focused on developing one of these – the linguistic. It is important to provide teaching and learning activities which engage with each 'intelligence' in order to support all types of learning need.

The following grid aims to help to get you started:

Knowledge of workings of the brain has begun to impact on approaches to teaching and learning

Intelligence type	Type of learner	Possible RE activities
Linguistic 	Good with words; enjoys reading, writing and listening, radio; explains things clearly; good at telling stories' enjoys poetry; likes word puzzles	• Reading and writing prayers, poems, faith and secular stories on spiritual or moral themes such as forgiveness, love, justice, peace • Using parable, myth, sacred text • Interpreting meaning from text and story
Logical/ mathematical 	Looks for reason and order; likes to calculate; good at maths; thinks logically; looks for pattern and links; makes lists; can be unwilling to compromise; can be obsessive	• Designing a diagram to represent the Noble Eightfold Path and what it means for everyday life • Designing a game to illustrate religious teaching • God arguments – looking at traditional reasons for believing • Looking at pattern in creation
Visual/ spatial 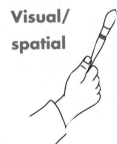	Likes to paint, draw, sculpt; pays attention to visual detail; good colour sense; good visual imagination; good at art; can 'read' pictures and video stills; good at ball games	• Interpreting the meaning of artefacts, paintings and symbols • Completing a picture, e.g. a Hindu murti in a home shrine • Designing a 'Hunger Cloth' to depict an aspect of the life and teaching of Jesus • Producing a 'Collage continuum' on the theme of good and evil
Bodily- kinaesthetic 	Uses hands and body to express ideas; needs to touch; likes sport; doesn't sit still much; likes crafts and model-making; good sense of balance; good co-ordination; enjoys walking and dancing; active; solves problems by experimentation	• Using drama, dance, mime and movement to express spiritual ideas and religious teachings and ritual • Grouping and regrouping for discussion

Intelligence type	Type of learner	Possible RE activities
Musical 	Likes to compose, sing and hum; plays an instrument; enjoys wide range of music; remembers tunes; sense of rhythm; taps out beat; sense of pitch; notices natural sounds; may be a good dancer	• Expressing religious ideas through singing and music • Interpreting or reflecting on songs and music • Exploring worship music • Action songs with younger children
Naturalistic 	Collection-type hobbies; groups, classifies, cross-references; may be a good organiser; keeps pets; observant; interested in all types of animal, insect, birdlife, dinosaurs, etc; enjoys watching nature programmes	• Reflecting and responding to order and pattern in the natural world • World faiths and 'green issues', e.g. concepts of ahimsa, stewardship • Wonder at creation
Interpersonal 	Relates well to others; enjoys company; team worker; has several close friends; good listener or counsellor; good at motivating people; club member; notices moods; concerned about people's feelings; enjoys parties	• Faith teachings on codes for living – looking for happiness • Activities relating to forgiveness and reconciliation, e.g. Yom Kippur (day of atonement in Judaism) • Developing active listening • Transforming encounters
Intrapersonal 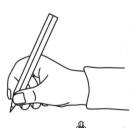	Knows self; self-motivated; determined; reflective; quiet; prefers to work alone; can appear shy; often keeps a personal diary; may daydream; a 'thinker'	• Activities which connect with the inner life of pupils, e.g. stilling, guided visualisation, reflecting on experience, exploring questions of meaning, reflective diaries, prayers or poems, getting 'inside' human experience

REtoday Services

Ato**Z**

Skill and attitude development in RE

RE is not only about content (learning about religions), it is also about response to that content (learning from religion). In order to raise standards of pupil achievement it is important to devise tasks and activities which enable pupils to develop the necessary skills and attitudes required in both aspects.

Skills: getting the balance right in RE

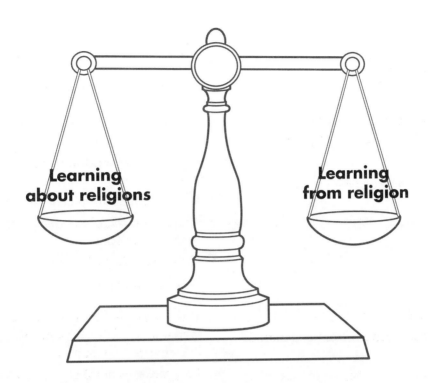

Learning about religions... **Developing knowledge and understanding about religions**	Learning from religion... **Enhancing own spiritual and moral development**

Key questions
What should pupils be able to know, understand and do?
 	
Focuses on...
Knowledge:
    fact
    description
    information
    investigation
Understanding:
    explanation
    interpretation
    analysis
    evaluation
	Key questions
	What opportunities are we providing for pupils to...
	
	• **consider** life's fundamental questions and how religious teaching relates to them?
	• **reflect** on their own beliefs and values in light of what they are studying in RE?
	• **express** learning, insight and experience?
	
	Focuses on...
	    reflection
	    application
	    interpretation
	    empathy
	    evaluation

Developing skills through active learning

The following grid suggests some possible active and experiential learning strategies for developing important skills in Religious Education. You will be able to add others.

The order of the skills is roughly hierarchical with lower order skills at the start and higher order skills towards the end. Increase the challenge of tasks by focusing on higher order skills of analysis, evaluation and synthesis.

RE teaching is intended to develop these skills	Examples of teaching and learning activities
Investigate This includes the ability to: • gather information from a variety of sources; • ask relevant questions; • know what may be appropriate information.	• Use a number of textbooks or websites to select information. • Highlight the important information on a handout. • Collect leaflets from churches, charities, etc. • Watch or listen and make notes from video, audio or website. • Write and ask for information. • Prepare questions for a visitor.
Apply This includes the ability to: • apply what has been learned from a religion to a new situation.	• Write a story to be acted out showing the meaning of a faith story or religious teaching in a different context. • Design own symbols. • Case study or dilemma – think about what Jesus, Guru Nanak, Buddha might do or say, what a Muslim might do, etc.
Empathise This includes the ability to: • consider the thoughts, feelings, experiences, beliefs and values of others; • see the world through someone else's eyes; • develop the power of the imagination to identify feelings such as love, forgiveness, sorrow, joy.	• Role-play and freeze-frame – drama and mime activities. • Feelings graph for one character (e.g. Peter in Holy Week). • Write captions to pictures or slides. • Tell a story or write a diary entry from another person's point of view. • Hotseat – answer questions in role of another person.
Interpret This includes the ability to: • draw meaning from, for example, artefacts, symbols, stories, works of art and poetry; • interpret religious language; • suggest meanings of religious texts.	• Talk about meaning in artefacts, pictures, paintings or symbols. • Respond to questions such as, 'What do you think it is?', 'What is going on?' (in a picture), 'What issues does the story raise?' • Use figures of speech or metaphors to speak about religious ideas. • Read prayers and talk about what they show about the person's beliefs and feelings.

RE teaching is intended to develop these skills	Examples of teaching and learning activities
Reflect This includes the ability to: • ponder on feelings, relationships, experience, ultimate questions, beliefs and practices; • think and speak carefully about religious and spiritual topics.	• Provide opportunities for pupils to describe how atmosphere and actions make them feel. • Take part in stilling or guided visualisation activities. • Use music to explore feelings and thoughts. • Write a prayer a Jewish, Christian or Muslim child might use. • Write a poem. • Keep a reflective diary. • Make a 'wall of wisdom' to record pupils' insights.
Express This includes the ability to: • explain concepts, rituals and practices; • identify and express matters of deep concern by a variety of means – not only through words; • respond to religious issues through a variety of media.	• *Creative* – drama, role-play, dance, mime, add percussion or actions to religious story or song, make a game. • *Visual* – use of collage, colour, charts, diagrams, video. • *Oral* – use of audio tape, presentation or debate. • *Written* – poetry, reflective diary, letter, narrative story, newspaper report, questions for interview or visit, etc.
Analyse This includes the ability to: • draw out essential ideas, distinguish between opinion, belief and fact; • distinguish between key features of different faiths; • recognise similarities and differences.	• Identify key words, beliefs, points of view in a text, faith story or website. • Match quotations to different faiths or perspectives studied. • Identify differences and similarities in religious beliefs and practices within and between different faiths studied.
Evaluate This includes the ability to: • draw conclusions by reference to different views and using reason to support own ideas; • debate issues of religious significance with reference to experience, evidence and argument.	• Use sorting and ranking strategies such as diamond-ranking statements according to what pupils think, or what a Muslim, Christian, Jew, Buddhist, Sikh, Hindu might think. • 'Can of worms' activity in which pupils give personal responses to statements relating to topics in RE. • Human barchart activities – pupils respond to points of view on a scale of 1–10, followed by discussion. • Debate.
Synthesise This includes the ability to: • link significant features of religion together in a coherent pattern; • make links between religion and human experience.	• Notice similarities between stories and practices from religions. • Talk about prayers, texts, places of worship, festivals – drawing conclusions about similar beliefs, values, practices. • Hypothesising, e.g. 'What if Muhammad or Jesus came to Britain today … what would he say and do?'

Attitudes

Religious Education should help pupils to develop a positive attitude:

- towards themselves;
- towards other people, respecting their right to hold different beliefs from their own;
- towards living in a religiously plural and multicultural society.

	The development of...
Self-understanding	<ul><li>a mature sense of self-worth, enabling pupils to be confident in their capacity to reflect and offer thoughtful insights and questions of meaning and purpose;</li><li>a strong sense of identity: confidence and appreciation of personal, family, cultural and religious values;</li><li>willingness to listen and consider views of others whilst not being readily swayed by them;</li><li>willingness to acknowledge the possibility of being wrong, biased or prejudiced;</li><li>personal integrity in living one's beliefs and values.</li></ul>
Fairness	<ul><li>a willingness to listen and give careful consideration to the views of others;</li><li>a willingness to consider evidence and argument;</li><li>a willingness to look beyond surface impressions.</li></ul>
Respect	<ul><li>recognition of the rights of others to hold views, beliefs and customs different to one's own;</li><li>the ability to discern between what is worthy of respect and what is not;</li><li>an appreciation that religious convictions are often deeply held.</li></ul>
Enquiry	<ul><li>the desire to explore deeper questions and search for answers to such questions;</li><li>an open mind which can wonder;</li><li>a willingness to learn from the insights of others and be prepared to reconsider existing views;</li><li>curiosity and desire to seek the truth.</li></ul>

Attitudes to learning

Some attitudes, such as fairness, respect and enquiry, are fundamental to RE in that they are prerequisites for entering into knowing and understanding about religions and learning from them.

Affirmation exercise

Useful for: developing self-esteem; encouraging sensitivity to others' feelings.

Number pupils 1–30 (or whatever, depending on the number in the group). Each pupil is given a sheet of paper and asked to write his or her name on the top line. The papers are passed to the next person (1 to 2, 2 to 3, and so on), who then writes a positive comment about the person on the bottom line. He or she folds the sheet up to hide the comment and passes it on to the next person. This continues around the room until everyone has his or her own sheet back.

This activity makes a good starter activity in RE when:

- introducing religious teaching on the special value of 'unique' individuals, for example the Christian concept that all are created in the image of God and precious to God;
- learning about Christian infant baptism, or welcoming and naming ceremonies in other faiths;
- exploring the importance of names when introducing the ninety-nine beautiful names of God (Islam).

Note: This exercise needs careful preparation to highlight the importance of honesty and sensitivity towards the feelings of others. It works best in a group in which there is trust and co-operation.

Agenda setting

What is the problem?

Who is affected?

Where does it happen?

Why does it happen?

How could it be tackled?

What is the best way **forward**?

Who will take **action**?

Useful for: structuring discussion; developing enquiry and analysis skills.

Devise an agenda of questions for small discussion groups, taking care to challenge pupils to address all the key aspects of the topic. These can also be used to guide research and enquiry outside the classroom

For example: Exploring conflict

Provide newspaper articles describing six real-life conflict situations. These are read out and pupils are asked to visualise what it is like for the real people in these situations. Divide pupils into six groups, each group taking one of the conflict scenarios. Analyse the problem using the questions listed on the left.

Follow-up discussion could focus on:

- Which of the above questions is the most difficult to answer? Why?
- Are there any causes of conflict that are common to all the situations?
- Have you experienced any of these causes of conflict in your own life?
- Who has to take action?

Agony aunts

Useful for: applying religious and moral teaching to contemporary situations.

Pupils even in primary schools will be familiar with the problem pages of teenage magazines. Writing and responding to letters of this type can encourage pupils to reflect on their own and others' worries, thoughts, feelings, needs and so on.

Dear ...,

I am a practising Hindu and have met a really nice boy at school. He's asked me to go to out with him. He's not a Hindu and I don't think my parents will let me go. I'm 15. What should I do?

Agree/disagree

Useful for: starter activity to a lesson or series of lessons.

Controversial statements are used to stimulate interest in the lesson content. Pupils who disagree with the statement move to one side of the room; those who agree move to the other. A continuation of this would be for pupils to form themselves into pairs or small groups with those on the same side to work out their argument for supporting their position on the issue.

See also: *Human bar chart* activity

For example: Why do people fight?

Controversial statements:

People who fight are no better than animals.

People have to fight to protect themselves, their belongings or their families.

It is always wrong to fight – violence only leads to more violence.

People who fight have guts, they are prepared to stand up for themselves and others.

AGREE

DISAGREE

Analysing a problem

Useful for: involving pupils in consideration of a problem which may have occurred in school or outside in society; taking pupils' insights and perspectives seriously; encouraging active participation in the resolution of the problem.

Discussion groups are formed and the following questions are addressed:

- What is the problem?
- Who does it affect?
- Where, when and why does it happen?
- How could it be tackled?
- What is the best way forward?
- Who will take action?
- How will the action be monitored and reviewed?.

For example: Racial prejudice

As part of a unit on religion, prejudice and discrimination, pupils identify a concern about racial prejudice in their own community. The above questions provide a framework for discussion and action planning.

AtoZ

Art work

Useful for: displaying concepts and ideas along with, or as an alternative to, written work; allowing self-expression and communication for those who find other areas of communication difficult.

This can take various forms: collage, freehand drawing, sculpture, printing, and so on.

See also: *Collage and collage continuum, Hunger Cloth.*

Banners

Banner for justice Banners are associated with protest marches against injustice. Produce a banner based on the trade justice theme, linked to work on Christian Aid or CAFOD, or base it on a quote from Martin Luther King Junior: 'Before you have finished breakfast today you have depended on half the world'.

Banner for freedom Pupils reflect on the meaning of Pesach (Passover) for Jews and produce a 'freedom banner' to express the joy and excitement of freedom after captivity.

LIFE BEFORE DEATH

FREEDOM OPEN YOUR WINGS AND FLY

Colour

Pupils are invited to express the feelings and insights stimulated by story, ritual or music through colour. For example, what might be the colours which capture: the experience of Pentecost; the Exodus crossing of the Red Sea; or the joy in creation, incarnation, celebration or praise?

Display

Pupils suggest and gather materials for such themes as:

* the beauty of creation and the natural world in connection with creation stories or harvest;
* good and evil;
* hope for the future;
* what is a human being?

Natural collage

Useful for: reflection; imaginative and creative expression of human experiences; stimulating discussion.

Use natural materials such as a branch of a tree or a flower stem to create a natural collage. Take a theme such as change, death and rebirth. Encourage pupils to express reflectively their own understanding of these concepts using the branch arranged on a sheet of sugar paper.

For example: This approach is a particularly effective way of expressing brokenness in human relations – and the cycle of remorse, confession, forgiveness and reconciliation.

* Give pupils something natural like a flower on a stem with leaves attached or a twig with leaves. Explain that this represents a person.
* Ask pupils to use the flower stem or twig to express the feelings of remorse, confession, forgiveness and reconciliation. Encourage pupils to think about how they can do this. (The branch or twig may start off whole, be broken, fragmented, or even crushed and then re-constructed to symbolically express the steps in the breakdown and rebuilding of human relationships.)

Art work (continued)

Picture extending

Useful for: finding out if pupils understand the context, use and purpose of religious artefacts; pupils who prefer visual forms of expression; getting pupils to talk about their understanding of religious artefacts.

Give pupils a section of a picture and ask them to finish it. Encourage pupils to think about:

- the setting they would normally expect to see the object in;
- other objects they associate with it which might also need to be in the picture;
- colours and symbols they associate with the object (and what these may mean).

Pupils can either write or give a brief verbal commentary on their picture.

Can you identify this
and complete the table for Shabbat?

Can you identify this object
and transform it into a home shrine
or add items used in worship in the mandir?

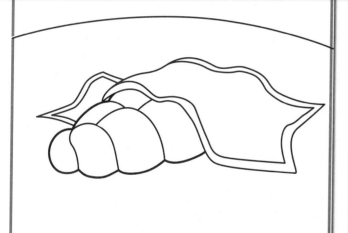

REtoday
Services

Artefacts

Artefacts, both religious and everyday, provide a wealth of stimulus material to actively engage pupils. It is important to remember, however, that religious artefacts must always be treated with respect because of their significance to the faith traditions concerned.

Christian ways of praying

You will need two prayer books, two icons and two rosaries. Divide the class into six groups. Two groups focus on an icon, two on the rosary beads and two on a prayer book. Each group responds to six questions:

- What is it?
- What is it made of?
- What is it used for?
- How is it used?
- What does it tell us about Christian belief about prayer?
- What questions do we want to ask about it?

One person from each group reports back to their half of the class.

This activity could be adapted for use with artefacts from other world faiths.

Give us a clue

Useful for: engaging pupils in reflection on the meaning of a religious artefact; a fun way of establishing prior knowledge and understanding and encouraging speaking and listening.

The teacher produces a mystery object. Pupils are asked to privately write down: (a) who they think might use or value this object; and (b) what they think it is. They write their name on the paper, fold it in half and hand it in.

Pupils then take it in turns to ask for clues and to make suggestions about the purpose and value of the artefact to a religious believer. Only when most pupils are agreed that they think they know the correct answers does the teacher tell them what the mystery object is and who uses it. Use the written answers to find out who knew the answer from the start.

Moebius strip

Useful for: stimulating a touch of mystery; encouraging reflection on perceptions and how we 'see' life; reflecting that things are not always what they appear to be.

A Moebius strip is a twisted loop, normally made of paper – it is unusual because it only has one side and one edge.

Make a long strip of paper by cutting an A4 sheet into three lengthwise and joining the ends. Hold as if to make a cylinder, then put in a half twist (180°) and stick together.

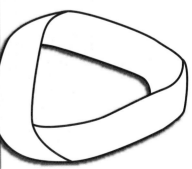

Use it as a visual aid. Ask pupils:

- How many sides has it got? (Draw a line down the middle and find out.)
- How many edges has it? (Mark a point on the edge and run your fingernail around it.)
- What do you expect to get if you cut along the line you drew down the middle of the paper?
- How could you use this as a visual aid to talk about the way religion sees the world?

Mystery bag

A cloth bag with a question mark on it and a drawstring top can be purchased or made. An artefact such as a chalice could be placed in the bag and passed around the group. Pupils are asked to feel it carefully, suggest adjectives to describe it, and, after reflection, guess what it is and how it might be used.

Natural objects

Useful for: a starter activity for exploring creation stories with younger pupils, or for work with older pupils in relation to religion and science or questions about God.

Give pupils the opportunity to focus and reflect on creation through natural objects – flowers, leaves, stones, shells.

- Ask pupils to choose one and look at it carefully.
- Do you think you could make that?
- Do you think anyone could make it?
- Where did it come from?

Older pupils could reflect on the questions raised by the beauty, structure, pattern and order in the universe – starting with a flower head. Questions to explore might be:

- How might a scientist who believed in God respond?
- What might an atheist scientist say?

Ask students what they know about Fibonacci numbers and explore together.

Simulation of a shrine

Set up in the classroom a simulation of a shrine used for worship (for example, a Buddhist or Hindu shrine) using the appropriate artefacts. (Note: Handling Hindu murti statues in the classroom is acceptable, as these are not consecrated.) Invite a Buddhist or Hindu into the class to talk about their shrine at home. Pupils look carefully at the shrine, listen to the visitor speaking about his or her worship and then write a short poem or piece of prose explaining their own attitudes to worship.

Balloon debate

Useful for: 'values clarification' – exploring what matters most; can be adapted so that the contents of the balloon are objects or abstract values rather than people.

Pupils imagine that they are crossing an ocean or desert in a hot air balloon with a range of different people (for example, brain surgeon, industrialist, teacher) as their companions. Halfway across, the gas supply runs out and they are forced to make decisions about which of their companions should be thrown out in order for the balloon to stay aloft.

See also: Values.

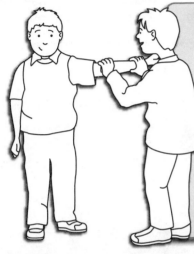

Body sculpture

Useful for: an active way of focusing pupils' thinking on the outward expression of inner feelings or attitudes – for example love, anger, hatred, forgiveness, injustice – as expressed by a narrative, text, poem, or video scene.

Pupils are paired. One takes on the role of the sculptor, the other the 'clay'. The sculptors 'mould' their partners to express the emotions or feelings they have identified in the stimulus material. Other pupils guess what inner feeling is being expressed. Photographing these could provide a useful starting point for discussion with other groups or make an interesting wall display.

Box story

- This activity, suitable for younger pupils, requires them to identify six main parts of a faith story.
- A picture with one or two key words is drawn on each side of a cube. These can either be drawn onto a template (see right) or pasted on to the sides of an existing box.
- Children can work individually or in groups.
- The completed box can be used for a game, throwing the box from one to another. Each time it is caught the catcher must tell that part of the story which is uppermost. A variation could be to play music and only when it stops does the pupil holding the box tell the story. (A variation of 'Pass the parcel'!)

For example: Biblical creation story; Rama Sita story; Hanukkah story; events of Holy Week.

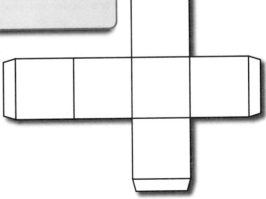

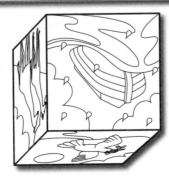

Brainstorming

Useful for: establishing existing knowledge and understanding; starter and plenary activities – if used at both ends this provides a useful insight into new learning acquired during a unit; generating new ideas; sorting ideas.

A key word or topic is selected; pupils list as many ideas as they can think of relating to it. No comment is made at this stage, the object being to 'get down' as many ideas as possible in as short a time as possible. On completion of the brainstorm, discussion – in pairs, groups or whole class – enables the ideas and issues identified to be sorted and prioritised and further thoughts and ideas sought as appropriate. Key issues for further research and discussion should also be identified.

For example: Year 4 pupils reflected on what freedom meant to them as part of a series of lessons exploring the significance of Pesach for Jews.

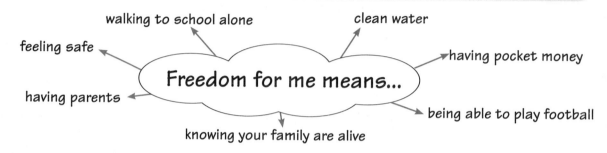

walking to school alone

clean water

feeling safe

having pocket money

Freedom for me means...

having parents

being able to play football

knowing your family are alive

Buzz groups

Useful for: focusing attention on key points and issues.

- Pupils are given two minutes to talk to one or two others about a specific topic or their reaction to something they have just seen or heard.
- It should be kept short and snappy to catch first reactions without getting involved in a full discussion.

For example: immediate responses to a speaker, a *PowerPoint* presentation or video clip.

Collage

Useful for: exploring issues which can be expressed in terms of a continuum between two opposites, for example good and evil, peace and war, love and hate, justice and injustice.

Using newspapers or colour supplements, pupils produce a collage on a given theme: for example, evil, crucifixion, love. Scissors are not always required as the act of tearing can be part of the process, and the rough edges symbolic.

For example: Goodness and evil collage continuum

Groups work together on a large piece of paper. Explain that one corner of the paper represents evil and the opposite corner represents good. The object of the exercise is for the group to work together to create a collage depicting a continuum or journey from the negative to the positive, using pictures, colours, symbols, words torn or cut out of magazines. The images express the group's ideas and feelings about the issues.

REtoday
Services

A to Z

Dance and movement

The body is an important medium of communication. As an alternative to drama or mime, dance and movement can be used to express spiritual or religious concepts, for example hope, forgiveness, love, compassion. Kinaesthetic learners enjoy expressing ideas through movement and gesture.

Why use dance and movement with children in RE?

Children can...

- learn about the story, belief or experience the dance communicates;
- talk about the meaning or importance of the story or belief to the believer;
- work out or ask questions about the meaning expressed in the movements.

How does it help children learn?

- We learn better when we are doing and taking part.
- Asking children to think about how they can express an idea in a movement or dance is a good strategy for getting pupils thinking, interpreting and expressing ideas.

Getting started with dance

There are always some people who do not want to join in dancing. They should not be made to do so, but everyone can help by suggesting ideas and planning. Also, those who do not dance can watch at the end.

1 Decide on a topic or theme for a dance. Some suggestions might be:
   - Use a story or a prayer (e.g. the Lord's Prayer).
   - Plan a dance around a piece of music or a painting relating to a religious festival or story.
   - Plan a dance around a universal theme such as happiness, celebration or freedom.
   - Use an idea from nature – growth, new life, seasons.

2 In small groups, work out the movements. Choose music carefully, if it is to be used. Rehearse the dance. Perform it to the rest of class or a wider audience, perhaps in assembly.

Developing understanding of religions through dance... ideas to get you started

God

Dance can offer a medium for expressing beliefs and ideas about God.

Pentecost

Pupils could work out short sequences to show God as a flame, a rushing wind, a dove, linked to the story of the start of the Christian church (the Bible, Acts 2).

Living prayer beads

Explore with pupils some of the ways in which believers describe God – perhaps the ninety-nine beautiful names in Islam, the Mool Mantar in Sikhism, Krishna in the Bhagavad Gita, or adjectives and metaphors used about God in the Christian and Jewish Bible. Perhaps as king, provider, creator, merciful, flame, light, father, shepherd, caring, prince of peace, judge. In pairs pupils could work out a gesture, stance or movement to demonstrate it. They could form a circle making a ring of 'living prayer beads', performing their movements one by one to express the key beliefs about God found in a particular faith.

Developing understanding of religions through dance... more ideas to get you started

Hinduism

- Use a video which shows Indian dance. Watch a scene with the soundtrack off. Ask pupils to pick out one hand, arm or eye movement, try to do it themselves and talk about what it might mean. Explain that Indian dance usually relates tales of gods and heroes of Hinduism – perhaps the story of Krishna stealing the butter or Rama reunited with Sita. See if anyone can guess what the story might be. Watch again with the sound up.

- In groups, pupils could work out some 'Indian' dance movements to express key moments in a Hindu story such as the Rama Sita story.

Judaism

Shabbat: A special day of freedom, peace and joy

- Dance: In groups, ask pupils to 'become' a repetitive machine. What sort of movements might they choose? How do they work together? This may be put to some suitable repetitive, 'mechanical' music. Then change the style of music to something much more free and fun. Encourage pupils to improvise and develop their own movements.

- Talk about how pupils felt in both dance activities. Did they feel more free, independent or creative in the second one? What would happen if they stayed in the first dance all the time?

Debate

Useful for: developing pupils' ability to employ argument and to anticipate and evaluate the arguments of others. There is a strong link here, and in other sections of this publication, with developing skills and attitudes outlined as part of the English PHSE and Citizenship framework for the primary school and the PHSE framework and Citizenship programme of study for the secondary school.

Pupils prepare a speech to argue for or against a motion, and others prepare short speeches 'from the floor' to lend support to one side. The speech is timed (5–6 minutes) and those from the floor should be no more than 2 minutes. At the end of the debate a vote is taken and the motion 'carried' or 'defeated'.

Note

- The motion needs to be carefully worded.
- Pupils need adequate time and support in preparing their speeches – it can be useful to enrol the help of colleagues in other curriculum areas.
- You need to have a 'fall-back' position worked out in case key participants are absent on the day, for example understudies prepared to stand in, key points for discussion ready.

Individuals should be given an opportunity to express their own considered opinion following the debate.

For example... Some possible motions for debate

- This house believes that money is the root of all evil.
- This house believes that prayer is answered.
- This house believes that abortion is wrong in all circumstances.

These are examples of a wide range of issues that could be debated.

See also: Human Barchart activity.

AtoZ

Diary entry

This empathetic exercise helps pupils to reflect on the feelings and experiences of characters within biblical (or other) stories. Careful follow-up activities enable pupils to reflect on such feelings in their own lives.

Singly or in pairs, pupils write pages of a diary for the different characters of a well-known story. Provide a writing frame to support less confident writers.

For example... The prodigal son (the Bible, Luke 15:11–32)

- The father – on the day his son left home.
- The friend – on the day the money ran out.
- The pig farmer – on the day the son asked for a job.
- The son – on the day he returned home.
- The brother – on the day his brother returned home.
- And what about the missing mother?

When completed, the pages are read out to the group.

This diary belongs to . . . .
Date: . . . .

Today . . . .
. . . .
. . . .

I felt . . . .
. . . .
. . . .

I knew I should . . . .
. . . .

I wanted to . . . .
. . . .

What I actually did was . . . .
. . . .
. . . .

I really hope . . . .
. . . .
. . . .

Diary of Reflection

Useful for: providing pupils with opportunities for quiet, structured reflection on issues of spiritual and moral worth or concern.

Many young people will be used to keeping diaries and writing confidential notes to friends. Here a similar means of self-expression is built into lesson activities. Usually the time spent on diary writing will be brief; often pupils are asked to complete a series of unfinished statements. The decision to share these inner thoughts and feelings is left to the pupil. Some will be happy to share ideas and often these stimulate thoughtful discussion. Basic ground rules need to be established at the start and confidentiality must be respected by all if pupils are to gain maximum benefit. The teacher provides the opportunity and creates the appropriate atmosphere.

Basic ground rules

- Diaries of Reflection are most effective when pupils are given regular opportunities to complete them in a quiet, disciplined exercise in an atmosphere of reflection.
- Unfinished statements are written on the board and used as a starting point. As pupils get more experienced with this activity, encourage them to suggest the starting points ... but always have some suggestions of your own ready.
- Confidentiality must be respected. No pupils' reflections must be read out or seen by other pupils, or teachers other than the class teacher, without the pupil's permission.
- Pupils should know that their diaries are valued and stored securely by the teacher.
- From time to time the teacher should write a positive, encouraging or questioning comment in response to one of the pupil's reflections.

When introducing Diaries of Reflection for the first time, it may be helpful to say something along the lines of the quotation to the left.

Your Diary of Reflection is an opportunity to stop your busy life for a few moments and think deeply about your own thoughts, feelings and beliefs. These moments will help you discover the most important directions and values in your life. They will help you to build a picture of the things that really matter to you and the kind of person you are becoming. Use them well and allow others to do the same.

Based on *Space for the Spirit* by Michael Beesley (Salisbury Diocesan Board of Education)

Discussion group strategies

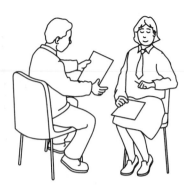

Planning for success

Think carefully about:
- what you want pupils to achieve (what learning outcomes? what task?);
- group size;
- classroom organisation and ground rules;
- seating arrangements;
- strategies for ensuring pupil co-operation and participation.

Task
- Pupils need to have a clear task and a clear timespan in which to work.
- They also need to have a clear picture of what they are going to do and what is expected of them, both in terms of outcomes and also how they are expected to go about the task.

Group size
- Paired work encourages all pupils to participate and is a good introduction to larger group work.
- Small groups should be no more than six pupils' four is better to ensure all take part.
- Use a range of strategies to group and regroup pupils – arranging for groups to regroup at key points enables pupils to have a new audience and hear others' ideas (see Rainbow groups and Jigsaw groups).

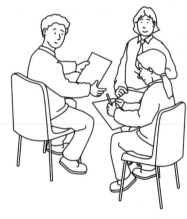

Classroom organisation and ground rules
- It may help to move desks back for some activities. Having desks facing outward to the wall for individual work, enabling chairs to be moved inwards for group work is an ideal arrangement – but not many classrooms are large enough for this.
- Negotiate ground rules before the activity begins – for example: only one speaker at a time; no offensive (e.g. racist or sexist) remarks; everyone should be listened to.

Seating arrangements

Pairs This can be a useful way of encouraging a more reserved pupil to share thoughts and feelings. It can be a first step to group discussion.

Trios This arrangement is useful when an observer or recorder is required. The roles should be rotated.

Small groups These can either be self-selected, selected randomly or a deliberately structured mix (gender or ability) by the teacher.

Whole class This provides a wider audience but can lead to less active participation from some. It will need chairing.

Circle within a circle This is a development from paired discussion. Pupils form an inner circle facing out opposite to a circle of pupils facing in. Pupils discuss their opinion with the partner opposite and then one circle moves round one place to bring everyone face to face with a new partner. This provides one-to-one discussion but with many different partners. It is confidence-building for the less self-assured and is clearly structured, providing support for learning.

Circle This allows everyone, including the teacher, to be an equal partner in the discussion. It encourages pupils to take the lead and everyone to discuss on an equal basis. Some way of identifying whose turn it is to speak is needed – by passing an object (see Pass the Orange) or identifying by name.

See also: Brainstorming; Human Barchart (a whole-class activity designed to afford pupils anonymity).

Strategies to get pupils talking

The following are some strategies designed to get everyone involved:

Can of worms

- Discussion questions on a particular theme (devised by either the pupils or the teacher) are written on slips of paper, cut up and placed in a jar.
- The jar is passed around the group, each person taking a question out and responding to it.
- Sentence completion is useful for this activity, for example:
    - 'I feel (angry) when...'
    - 'My idea of heaven is...'
    - 'My hope for the world is...'
- When using this with a 'circle within a circle', pupils on the inside pick out a question each, the outer circle rotates, the pupil asks the same question to each partner, noting down opinions for later feedback to the group as a whole. Outer and inner circles swap roles halfway through the activity.

Envoys

This is a way of sharing what has been discovered during group work without whole-class feedback.

After group work has been completed, one person is chosen to be an 'envoy'. The envoy moves to a new group to explain and summarise the findings of his or her own group and to find out what the new group thought, decided or achieved. The envoy returns to his or her own group and reports back.

Interviewing

Useful for: researching moral, social and religious issues; developing evaluation, speaking, listening and social skills.

- Suitable for researching and questioning an issue in pairs.
- Divide the class into two – one half are to be interviewers, the other interviewees. As a preparation homework, interviewers devise questions to ask and interviewees research the issue and work out their opinion on it.
- An interviewer is paired with an interviewee, asks their questions, and gets the responses, making a brief record (tape recording could be used). Repeat up to five times.
- The interviewers analyse the responses, synthesise the information and summarise the opinions of the interviewees (possibly for homework).
- The interviewees meet together in groups to share their findings on the issue, clarify their opinions, identify similarities and differences of opinion. Interviewers report back to the rest of the class. For the next issue, reverse the roles.

Jigsaw discussion

Useful for: ensuring participation from all pupils; developing speaking and listening skills.

- A topic is divided into sections. In home groups of four or five pupils, allocate sections to each and then regroup into expert groups i.e. the home group splits so that individual members go to different expert groups.
- The expert groups work on their aspect and then rejoin their home group to report back.
- The home group is then set a task, drawing on the different areas of expertise.

For example... Pupils use jigsaw strategy to compile a group dossier on Christian forgiveness, using case studies such as Philip Lawrence, Amy Biele, Corrie Ten Boom, Martin Luther King, and addressing the following key questions :

- What was there to forgive?
- Why would it have been hard to forgive?
- Why did the person forgive?
- What would have been the alternatives?
- What effect did forgiving have?

See also: Hunger Cloth activity; Jigsaw (Conjoined twins dilemma) for further examples.

Strategies to get pupils talking

The following are some strategies designed to get everyone involved:

Pass the orange

Useful for: both primary and secondary – a structured variation of primary circle time activities.

- Pupils sit in a circle. One person is given a large orange (or similar item).

- A discussion starter is read out. Only the person with the orange can comment. At first use non-threatening topics for discussion such as 'watching television'. As the class gains confidence topics can become more 'personal' or controversial.

- Everyone must give the person speaking their full attention. When he or she has finished the orange is passed to the next person, who comments on the original statement or a previous speaker's observations on it.

- Use a structure such as 'I agree/disagree with X because...'

- Regular use of this activity will encourage participation and openness.

Rainbow groups

Useful for: regrouping pupils in an easily manageable way; helping pupils learn from the findings of a range of other pupils.

- After small-group activity, each member of the group is given a number or colour. All pupils with the same number or colour re-form into new groups.

- In the new groups, pupils take it in turns to report back on the findings and achievements of their previous group.

For example: Pupils explore religious beliefs about marriage in groups with a focus on one religion. On completion the groups are reorganised. The task of the new group is to identify similarities and differences in the beliefs and teaching of the religions studied. This activity works well with examination classes, supporting informed and evaluative essay writing.

Snowballing

- Pupils are presented with a question, dilemma or issue for discussion.

- Each pupil shares his or her thoughts with a partner.

- The pair combines with another pair; they agree a group opinion or plan of action and either appoint a spokesperson to give a brief report back to the class as a whole, or use the plan of action to complete the task.

For example: Pupils are exploring religious teaching on rules for living. Individually pupils are given the 'rules for living' for one religion. They reflect on what they agree with or think is important; and anything they disagree with or don't understand. Next, in pairs they exchange ideas and write down three 'codes or rules for living' which they think matter most from the examples provided. Next in groups of four or six they compare and sort their ideas, identify 'rules for living' they wish to recommend to the class and appoint and brief a spokesperson. Whole-class feedback from the groups follows. Key questions are posed for discussion, such as 'Are there some principles that all groups agreed on?' and 'If we are agreed that these are good rules to live by – do we actually live by them?'

Statement response

Useful for: enabling full participation; ensuring anonymity; encouraging thoughtful personal opinions to be expressed in writing.

- A story, article or case study is read to raise an issue or reveal attitudes.

- In response to a specific question, for example 'Is it always wrong to take human life?', pupils write their views on slips of paper.

- These are collected in and read out.

A to Z

Drama

The body is an important medium of communication. Drama or mime can be used not only to demonstrate pupils' understanding of religious stories and rituals, but also to express spiritual or religious concepts such as reconciliation, life as journey, resurrection. Use of drama is a particularly good approach for those pupils who learn best by doing rather than writing.

See also: Role-play; Freeze-frame; Mime; Hotseating; Transporting a character.

Sacred literature as drama

Useful for: enabling pupils to interpret and express their understanding of the meaning of the text.

Sacred writings contain some of the richest dramatic texts and their stories are often acted out in dance and drama during festivals. For example:

- The story of the Nativity – Christmas, Christianity.
- The story of the Exodus – Passover, Judaism.
- The story of Esther – Purim, Judaism.
- The story of Rama and Sita – Diwali, Hinduism.

Ritual as sacred drama

Within religious worship there are rituals which form sacred drama. For example:

- the communion service in Christianity;
- the seder meal in Judaism.

Whilst these are open to study and representation, care must be taken not to trivialise them.

As in any dramatic activity, pupils must be encouraged to think themselves into the part – in this case, that of the reverent worshipper within the faith community. This is not encouraging children to worship, but to behave as if they were worshippers for the purpose of getting inside a faith.

E-mail from ...

Useful for: focusing pupils' thinking, opening up dialogue and drawing attention to contrasting perspectives; giving pupils a chance to respond to each other's work.

Electronic mail (e-mail) provides pupils with an opportunity to access the 'authentic voice' of the believer and to understand that religious expression and belief are real, contemporary and important to people in the local, national and international community. E-mail can support learning in RE in a variety of ways and in all key stages. The conventions of e-mail are quite informal, the register of writing often brief and to the point. Composing and drafting the e-mail message helps pupils clarify what they wish to ask or the view they want to express. For example, pupils could:

- devise a question for an 'expert' about a religion they are studying, and send it as a class e-mail;
  - e-mail local places of worship to gather information about them;
    - communicate with pupils from other faith traditions in 'partner' schools. (For further information, see *Building E-Bridges* by Julia Ipgrave, RE Today Services, 2003.)

This simple idea can also be used in many creative ways, with pupils writing e-mails from the past, from the future, from the angels, from heaven or hell, from a particular country or situation or in a particular ethical dilemma.

For example... An e-mail from the past

After a study of the last week of Jesus' life, pupils are allocated different characters within the story, e.g. Peter, Judas, Simon of Cyrene, Mary, and asked to write a short e-mail message, describing and explaining what they know, and suggesting questions which they have. Pairs of pupils then swap the messages, and answer each other..

Everybody up!

Useful for: a fun starter activity to get the whole class involved and thinking. It engages reflection on personal responses to a situation or an issue as a starting point for further exploration.

Ask the class to stand up. Tell pupils to 'stay standing if...' At this point, have ready a series of statements connected to a particular topic. Everyone who has done this, thought this, wondered this at any time stays standing; everyone else sits down. When a few are left standing, the teacher or a pupil interviews one or two people about their experiences.

For example... Exploring the issue of wealth and poverty

Stay standing if you have ever...

- asked your mum or dad for extra money.
- felt as though you were really missing out because you hadn't got the latest...
- thought beggars should be cleared off the streets.
- felt a bit guilty eating your tea watching starving people on the news.
- put a pound (or a penny) in a charity box.
- known someone who has tried to do something about the poor.

REtoday
Services

Freeze-frame

Useful for: enabling pupils to 'get inside the story' to explore the feelings and experiences of key characters; developing skills of analysis, empathy and expression; developing group work and speaking and listening skills.

This activity requires pupils to set up a scene as if it were a video freeze-frame or a still from a play. It is a co-operative activity which most pupils enjoy and find non-threatening.

For example... Freeze-framing a faith story

- Having heard or read a faith story, pupils, in groups, are asked to identify a key moment or turning point in the narrative. They then identify which characters are involved, allocate roles and discuss what each might be thinking and feeling at the key moment.

- Together they work out and 'act out' a 'freeze-frame' or 'still' image to depict the scene.

- The teacher touches the shoulder of an individual who then shares the thoughts and feelings of their character 'in role'. Pupils can also ask questions of the character 'in role' – this is a version of the 'hotseating' pupils may have tried as a literacy activity.

- Use of a digital camera to record 'freeze-frames' enables pupils to reflect on and record the thoughts and feelings of characters in speech bubbles and add these to the image.

Games

The following general games may be adapted for different classroom purposes:

Boardgames

Useful for: helping pupils reflect on their goals in life; reflecting on the realities of living. This activity links well with work on Hinduism and for reflection on the qualities that make up a 'good' person, e.g. St Paul's 'fruit of the spirit' – love, joy, etc. (the Bible, Galatians 5:22–23).

Using the basic idea of a simple boardgame such as Snakes and Ladders, pupils design a game on an RE theme, for example 'Journey of Life'.

For example: Snakes and Ladders originates in the Moksha Chitram game from India. It is about the ups and downs of life. Its aim is to aid reflection on things which help and hinder a person's progress through life to the ultimate goal of release from the cycle of births and rebirths. Pupils could devise their own version of this game.

- First of all, pupils identify goals, values and hopes they have for life.

- Next, pupils list any difficulties, challenges and negative attitudes which might prevent attainment of these goals, values and hopes.

- Finally, pupils make a playing board. Do this by drawing a grid of 100 squares and then drawing in symbols and illustrations to represent equal numbers of 'positive' and 'negative' items identified during earlier discussion, across the board. Ladders are then added to link some of the positive values to the goals and some snakes to link difficulties with movement down the board. Pupils play the game in the same way as Snakes and Ladders.

Games (continued)

> **Not Such a Bad Thing**

Pretty Lousy

Bad Enough

Still Bad

Really Bad

Awful

Dreadful Evil

Hideous and Appalling Evil

The Worst Evil of All

Sorting, ranking and discussion games

For example... The Evil Game

Useful for: helping pupils to think and clarify their ideas about the concept of evil; make decisions about what they jointly consider to be the greatest evil; present their own ideas and listen to the ideas of others, developing their speaking, listening and negotiating skills.

Pupils are given a pack of cards in which each card identifies one form of evil in the world. Each pupil takes five cards at random and, taking turns, places them on a ranking board, ranging from 'pretty lousy' to the 'most evil thing in the world'. Pupils place the cards only after explanation, discussion and negotiation with the rest of the group.

(See *Developing Secondary RE: Evil and Goodness*, edited by Joyce Mackley, RE Today Services, 2002, ISBN 1–904024–20–3).

Games adapted from TV and radio

Mystery words

This game, based on the TV programme *Call My Bluff*, is a fun way of introducing or reinforcing new vocabulary. For each word, offer two or three descriptions, only one of which is true. This can be done by splitting the group into two teams. Each group has two or three new words and right and wrong answers. After group A reads out the word and the possible answers, group B has to decide which is the right definition.

Just a minute

Useful for: getting pupils talking at the start of a new topic; drawing together learning at the end of a topic.

This activity is based on the long-running radio programme. Pupils have to speak for a minute on a given topic (for example, things to be thankful for, the importance of Christmas, saying sorry, what matters most in life, life after death, good and evil) without hesitation, deviation or repetition. Points are awarded to the challenger for a correct challenge and the challenger takes over the speaking. Points are awarded to the speaker for an incorrect challenge and for being the one who is speaking when the 60 seconds are up. An extra point is given to the speaker if they complete the 60 seconds without being successfully interrupted.

Through the keyhole

In this TV programme, viewers find out about a mystery person by looking in their house.

Ask pupils to think of things in their bedroom that show it is theirs.

Get pupils to play 'Through the keyhole' as a class. In pairs they can choose four things in their bedroom that identify them. The teacher can make this into a quiz, giving items from one pupil's list, and seeing who can guess whose it is.

Use the 'Through the keyhole' approach to find out about a Hindu, Sikh or Christian home and family. For example a Hindu family home might contain: murtis or images of gods and goddesses; an arti tray; a copy of the Bhagavad Gita; Divas, lamps used to celebrate Diwali; Rakhis, wristbands given by siblings at Raksha Bandhan. For each item, explore with pupils what it tells us about the person 'who lives in a house like this'.

REtoday
Services

A to Z

Gift for life

Useful for: a starter activity before going on to explore what, for believers, is 'the gift' which God offers them, for example: Jesus; gifts of the Spirit; Allah, the giver of life and health.

- Give everyone two sheets of paper. Ask them to write down in the middle of one the word 'Gift'.
- Brainstorm everything which comes to mind. Ask the pupils to cross out any words which are things money can buy. Ask them to focus on 'gifts' which money cannot buy – spend one or two minutes in quiet reflection.
- Using the other sheet of paper, pupils write down, and illustrate if they want, something they would like to give the person on their left to 'help them on their journey of life'. Allow a few minutes and then ask everyone to pass on their gifts.

Follow-up discussion: What gifts were received? What are their thoughts about their gift?

Guided visualisation

Useful for: getting inside faith stories, engaging pupils' imaginations and feelings, developing empathy.

This involves the teacher guiding the pupils through an imaginative visualisation. After a period of **stilling** (see page 60), the teacher begins to construct a scene and slowly guides the pupils though it. The aim is to engage the imagination and feelings. An essential aspect is the debriefing period immediately following the exercise, during which the teacher provides opportunities for participants to explore how they felt and what they experienced. Activities follow which allow pupils to express and develop their insights. Scripting biblical stories as guided visualisations is a good way of engaging pupils imaginatively with the events of the story.

Note: Guided visualisation is a valued educational strategy when focused on 'getting inside' faith stories or exploring positive aspects of experience. The classroom is not the right place to invite pupils deliberately to encounter painful or darker experiences, although these too may be important aspects of spiritual experience.

See also: Scripts for guided visualisations are to be found in many sources, including *Don't Just Do Something, Sit There* by Mary Stone (RMEP, 1995, ISBN 1-85175-105-X).

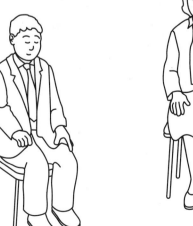

Guidelines for using guided visualisation

Before

- When using guided visualisation for the first time with a group, ask for co-operation and invite pupils to share responsibility for what happens. Start small; don't expect them to be able to participate in an extended activity from the word go.
- Seek to create the right atmosphere. Think about the positioning of furniture – should participants sit in a circle? Do the blinds need drawing? Should you have music playing in the background? Would a lighted candle provide a useful focus point?
- Have an alternative activity ready in case things don't go to plan.
- Think about how you can best help participants to feel secure and comfortable. Tell them that if at any time they start to feel uncomfortable they can open their eyes and stop taking part (whilst not stopping others from doing so, of course).
- Negotiate ground rules for the group.
- Minimise the risk of interruption, e.g. put a note on the outside of the classroom asking not to be disturbed.

During

- Start in a clear, reassuring way. Be confident, speak firmly, be in charge of the activity. Tell the pupils what to do.
- Allow for 'opt-out', 'non-active participation', 'the observer role', but without disturbing others (fundamental ground rule).
- Begin with a stilling exercise. For example: Sit up, both feet on the floor, hands together on lap or one hand on each knee. Breathing (normal at first, then a little slower and deeper), listening (to sounds outside the room, inside the room, the breathing of the person who is sat next to you, your own breathing), relaxing, self-awareness.
- Speak calmly and don't forget to allow appropriate pauses in the narrative.
- Keep an eye on the time – allow plenty of time for debriefing and follow-up.
- Finish by inviting them: 'When you are ready, open your eyes...', stretch (sensibly – another ground rule) and relax.
- Do not allow talking immediately (ground rule), let there be a short pause or silence.

After

The follow-up activity or activities should be given about the same amount of time as the guided visualisation. Activities could include:

- creative work (drawing, painting);
- writing (poetry, Diary of Reflection, summary note);
- drama (role work, mime, freeze-frame, dance);
- discussion (paired, small-group, whole-class).

Pupils should be free to share their thoughts, feelings and experience of the guided visualisation or not – no one should be forced to (ground rule).

Follow-up discussion (paired, small-group or whole-class) must ensure that:

- pupils are given adequate time to share ideas, thoughts and feelings;
- pupils are encouraged to listen carefully and sensitively to the ideas, thoughts and feelings of others;
- pupils are helped to articulate their learning through the experience.

REtoday
Services

Example script for a guided visualisation: Jesus is baptised

I want you to imagine that you are sitting near a river. It's a very hot day. You look for somewhere shady out of the heat. You look out over the river ... at the cooling water ... listen to the sounds it makes.

You are miles away from anywhere, but you are not alone. Nearby are the friends you made as you travelled from Nazareth. You had to come, you had to find out for yourself. Everyone was talking about this man John. People said he could wash away all the things you were sorry for ... give you a new start.

Look ... there's John now ... can you see him? He's standing in the river, up to his waist in water. He looks thin and scrawny ... his long hair resting on his scruffy cloak tied with a leather belt. There's a man standing next to him ... he looks familiar. Wait a minute ... you know him. He's the carpenter from Nazareth ... Joseph's son ... You want to shout to him ... to ask him ... What do you want to ask him?

John recognises him too ... he seems to be saying something to him. What do you think John might be saying? Next thing you know, Jesus is coming up out of the water. Look at his face ... he looks so peaceful ... so serene. He seems to be listening to something ... or someone. (Who or what do you think it might be?)

Somehow you know something very important has happened ... you feel it's something you'll never forget. Spend a few minutes going over all that's happened.

And now we're going to leave Palestine and return to our classroom ... Feel the hardness of the chair under you ... wriggle your toes ... take a long slow breath ... and when you're ready ... open your eyes.

Follow-up activities

- Provide pupils with cut-out speech bubbles. Ask them to focus on one person in the story and write down something that person might have felt, thought or said. Choose another character and do the same for that person.

- Use these to talk about the event – Who was involved? What was happening? How did Jesus feel? Who was John? What did he do? Why did he do this? Did this remind you of a special ceremony some Christians go through today?

- Pupils could write a diary entry for the day from the point of view of one person in the story.

Hotseat

Useful for: consolidating learning; developing questioning skills, speaking and listening; a diagnostic activity for use in assessment.

One member of the group sits centrally and can be asked any question from the floor which they answer from the perspective of a specified role. Teachers and other adults can be in the hotseat, answering in role or for themselves. Pupils should not be required to answer for themselves.

Examples

- **A visitor** In the hotseat 'for real'. Pupils prepare questions in advance.
- **Questioning a character** A pupil takes the role of a character studied, for example Martin Luther King, Mahatma Gandhi, a disciple of Jesus (e.g. Peter or Judas). With younger pupils this can conclude a unit of work, pupils working together to work out questions to ask and answers to give if they are in the hotseat. With older pupils this activity follows careful preparation – pupils may submit questions to the person in the hotseat (and his or her group of advisers) in advance so that they may do some research. Pupils' questions must arise from their own research.
- **Beat the teacher** Pupils are asked to research and prepare questions to ask the teacher. They may work individually or in teams. When asking factual questions pupils must know the answers to the questions. Teams may compete to see which is able to 'beat the teacher'.

Human barchart

Useful for: developing discussion and evaluation skills. It encourages expression of personal viewpoints whilst respecting privacy, and enables pupils to see arguments from other people's perspectives. It works well with both older primary and secondary pupils.

This activity provides a structure which enables pupils to think about and express their own point of view on a series of controversial statements on a given topic. They do this privately and confidentially. These views are then represented by others in a visual way with pupils standing in lines to form a human barchart to show the range of opinion held in the class. A variation enables debate to follow with groups working together to develop arguments to support or oppose the viewpoint.

The activity requires the teacher to devise an opinions statement sheet made up of at least six controversial statements on the issue in question – see the opposite page for examples. Before the lesson begins, write the numbers 1–10 on A4 sheets and place them in a straight line on the floor or the wall of the classroom or corridor.

- Give pupils a sheet with a number of viewpoints on it about the topic you are exploring.
- Ask them to complete it privately and in pencil. Pupils circle the number which most closely reflects their opinion for each statement. 1 means strongly agree and 10 means strongly disagree. Encourage pupils to express their honest opinions by reassuring them that their responses will be completely anonymous.
- Each sheet is then folded in half and half again, and exchanged five times.
- As the teacher reads out the statements, pupils line up in front of the number represented on the sheet they have been given, creating a human barchart!

Pupils in each group, for example all those with 1 circled on their sheets, work out arguments to support the point of view they are representing. A good debate can arise between those who are 'strongly agreeing' with those who are 'strongly disagreeing'.

REtoday
Services

A to Z

Example opinions statement sheets

For primary pupils

Wise words

Strongly agree   **Strongly disagree**

Never try to get back at someone who makes you cry.

1   2   3   4   5   6   7   8   9   10

Worrying about what might happen is a waste of time.

1   2   3   4   5   6   7   8   9   10

If you fight you will get hurt by fighting.

1   2   3   4   5   6   7   8   9   10

Don't be greedy. Having lots of things won't make you safe and happy.

1   2   3   4   5   6   7   8   9   10

For secondary pupils

Forgiveness

Strongly agree   **Strongly disagree**

If you 'turn the other cheek' people will think you are a pushover.

1   2   3   4   5   6   7   8   9   10

Forgiveness is the principal quality of a civilised person.

1   2   3   4   5   6   7   8   9   10

Forgiveness gets the poison out of the system and allows us to get on with life.

1   2   3   4   5   6   7   8   9   10

Forgiveness is soft – it lets people get away with what they've done wrong.

1   2   3   4   5   6   7   8   9   10

Happy are those who forgive.

1   2   3   4   5   6   7   8   9   10

Life is a matter of getting even – not letting people get away with it.

1   2   3   4   5   6   7   8   9   10

Hunger cloth or Lenten veil

A hunger cloth is a Catholic community's prayer for their world represented in picture form. Many of these come from Central and South American Catholic communities. The cloths contain symbols and themes for Christians to study and think about during Lent. Many have a design layout which can be emulated for classroom work.

Classroom application

- Show an image of the hunger cloth on OHT or an actual cloth if available, revealing a little at a time – asking pupils what they see, what they think it means and what they think it is about.

- Explore the idea behind hunger cloths. Discuss how an issue, a faith story, or a religious teaching might be depicted visually. (What colours, symbols, images?)

- Set pupils the task of producing a hunger cloth design. Follow these steps:
  - Identify a religious issue or teaching, for example Christian teaching on justice or forgiveness.
  - As a class activity, talk about which key aspects should be depicted in the sections of the cloth.
  - In groups of five or six (depending on the number of sections in the cloth) each member is allocated a particular section to work on. Pupils move into 'specialist' groups to work out with others what their given aspect might include before returning to their own group to complete the design.
  - **For example...** A 'cloth' focusing on the theme of forgiveness might include sections on: Jesus' teaching, e.g. Sermon on the Mount; Jesus' actions, e.g. the healing of the paralysed man; a modern example of Christian forgiveness; images to depict a world without forgiveness; and an outcome of forgiveness, with symbols of love and harmony.

REtoday
Services

A to Z

Icebreakers

Useful for: getting to know a new class; introducing pupils to active strategies; providing a first opportunity to talk about some ground rules for active strategies in the classroom.

These are short activities designed to break down barriers, introduce people and encourage participation.

For example... **Circle games and name games**

Everyone who...

One person in the centre of the circle shouts out a statement and everyone to whom it applies changes places. Examples: 'Everyone who has a cat,' 'Everyone who loves (or hates) football.'

See also: Everybody up!

Getting to know you

- Everyone takes it in turn to introduce him- or herself by choosing and doing an alliterative action, for example dancing Duncan, sitting Sam. This could be followed up with the next activity.

- The teacher calls out categories of people, for example: people who play sport; people who play a musical instrument; people who don't like *Neighbours*. Anyone belonging to the category goes and sits in the middle of the circle. If they belong to the next category they stay in; otherwise they return to their seats. This could be linked to the seven aspects of intelligence, e.g. people who like puzzles (mathematical); people who like acting (kinaesthetic); people who like listening to others' problems (interpersonal). This might be an early clue to pupils' preferred learning styles.

I am

Useful for: a group that knows each other well; a starting point for work on symbol in religion or looking at ways of expressing what God is like.

Each member of the group is given a piece of card and asked to write or draw four things which symbolise themself – for example a football, a pet, a swimsuit, a pizza. When everyone is finished the cards are collected, shuffled and redistributed. Pupils take it in turns to 'interpret' the symbols and words to work out who the card is describing.

A variation could be to ask pupils to mime themselves holding the objects and to talk about what they might need to hold four things at once (extra hands?) This prepares children for looking at Hindu murtis with many arms and hands symbolising the characteristics of God.

Interviews

Interviewing a visitor or conducting a series of interviews to gather facts or opinions from a variety of people can be a worthwhile experience for pupils in trying to assimilate information and synthesise ideas. Interviews can be conducted in role (as a newspaper reporter or radio journalist).

Note: The success of this kind of exercise depends crucially on the interviewer having researched the topic thoroughly and developed appropriate questions which will elicit the required information. A key question which all interviewers should be clear about is what it is they are trying to find out.

See also: Discussion group strategies (Interviewing).

In the news

Useful for: application of religious teaching to contemporary situations; comparing contemporary religious interpretations with original teachings.

Pupils are asked to bring in newspaper cuttings which illustrate how beliefs affect actions in today's world. These will be both positive and negative.

For example... terrorist bombings, expressing the belief of a minority that human life can be sacrificed for political purposes; a person giving a kidney to save the life of another, expressing the belief in altruism and caring for others.

Ask pupils to decide what beliefs lie behind the actions. Consider how religion can be used for evil as well as good. Research original teachings to analyse whether the actions in the name of religion are consistent with these original teachings.

Further development: The activity 'Transporting a character' could be used to reflect on how, for example, Jesus, the Prophet Muhammad ﷺ, Mahatma Gandhi, Guru Nanak or Buddha might respond to particular events 'in the news' today.

Jigsaw activities

Revealing a picture

Useful for: a starter activity using a visual stimulus; establishing earlier learning or consolidating learning at the end of a unit; encouraging active participation.

A picture of a religious leader, artefact or a scene from a faith story is shown on an interactive whiteboard screen and slowly revealed using the 'blind' tool, or shown on an OHT and covered with jigsaw pieces. The picture is revealed bit by bit with pupils guessing the picture beneath and telling the class about the person or story it is about.

For example... Who are you?

After completing a unit of work on religious founders and leaders, have a picture of one religious leader on an OHT, covered with a piece of paper cut into jigsaw-type pieces.

Pupils are divided into teams of four. Each team in turn is asked a question from the work covered. A section of the picture is uncovered for each correct answer and the team given the chance to identify the person. The team which correctly identifies the person wins.

The game can be extended by continuing with another religious leader and totalling up the number of correct identifications each team has made at the end. The activity could be adapted to a range of content, e.g. places of worship, religious artefacts, holy books.

Jigsaw reading

Useful for: co-operative working and engaging pupils with the text so that they have to discern its meaning.

A piece of text is cut up into a number of pieces, muddled and given out to a group. Pupils read out each section and decide together the correct order of the pieces. These are then stuck onto a sheet of paper.

For example...

A faith story is rewritten into sections and printed onto card. Try this with stories such as Muhammad ﷺ in the cave (Islam), the walk to Emmaus (the Bible, Luke 24:13–32), or the founding of the Khalsa (Sikhism).

A narrative account of a moral dilemma is developed from news accounts, providing a range of moral and religious viewpoints. The example opposite uses the case of Jodie and Mary, the co-joined twins born to Roman Catholic parents in 2000.

The activity is suitable for secondary pupils and uses the following strategies:

* group work;
* jigsaw reading;
* jigsaw discussion grouping;
* role-play.

Secondary activity:
Should doctors or parents decide if one conjoined twin should die so the other can live?

Task

- In groups of four, sort the following statements to reconstruct the story of this religious and moral dilemma, establish lines of argument and work out who you think said what and why.
- After sorting the story line, allocate one of the following roles to each of the four members of the group:
  - the priest (the Roman Catholic position);
  - the judge (the legal position);
  - the professor of ethics (the ethical position);
  - the commentator (the observer's point of view).
- Regroup into specialist groups (i.e. all the 'priests' together) to do further research to help each other prepare for a role-play discussion.
- Return to your home groups. Role-play the discussion between the priest, the judge and the professor, with the commentator acting as observer and recorder. Each group feeds back, through the observer, the main issues and points raised.

Statements for sorting

The court should have allowed the parents to decide.	If there is no operation, it is likely both children will die.	Either decision is a tragic decision. If they decide to leave God's will to happen then both children will die.
We leave it in the hands of God. We have no right, no power about life. Life is in the hands of God.	When we start as humans deciding who lives and who dies ... I feel very uncomfortable.	The question is simple – do you kill one to save the other, or do you let two die?
If they decide to intervene or let the doctors intervene, then they will in effect be responsible for the death of one of the children in order to save the other.	For their parents, the operation is not a question of life or death. It is a test of their faith.	Two baby girls joined at the lower abdomen lie entwined in a hospital incubator in Manchester. One must die so the other can live.
As Roman Catholics they believe that it is wrong to do evil – sanctioning the death of a child – even though it could result in good.	These parents do not have weird views. They have very standard views, the most important of which is you don't kill one person in order to save another.	I think it's wrong. I think this is a classic example of a moral dilemma where two standard positions are in a clashing situation.
The pain of being on the sharp horns of this dilemma is excruciating because you do worry – and you do your best.	If there is hope one of them can survive, they can separate and let one live.	Whose job is it to decide questions of life or death? The court's. Not a job we ask for, but a job we have to do, most certainly.

Kaleidoscope

Useful for: exploring pattern and symmetry as an introduction to looking at issues of beauty and diversity in nature leading to questions of origins.

This optical instrument contains 2–4 reflecting surfaces placed in a tube, at one end of which is a container holding coloured glass. Looking into the kaleidoscope, a person sees a rainbow of brightly coloured symmetrical patterns that can be changed by turning the end of the tube.

- In groups, pupils take it in turn to look into a kaleidoscope and explain what they see.
- Use ideas about pattern and symmetry in nature to lead into discussion about how, or by whom, that beauty and diversity was 'created' and is sustained.
- Pupils can be asked to look for pattern and symmetry in nature. Use a website such as *Religion, Pattern and Meaning in Nature* (to be found via http://re-xs.ucsm.ac.uk/re/pattern.html).

Kitchen

Food plays an important role in religion.

- Foods are associated with religious festivals and holy days: for example, hot cross buns for Christians at Easter, potato latkes for Jews at Hanukkah, challah loaves and wine at Shabbat.
- Food plays an important part in religious worship rituals and ceremonies: for example, karah prasad, a specially cooked sweet pudding blessed through prayer in the presence of the Guru Granth Sahib and then distributed to Sikh worshippers; bread and wine shared during holy communion, Eucharist or Lord's supper in Christianity.
- Dietary laws often reflect beliefs about creation and about humanity's relationship with the created world, with each other and with God. Kashrut (kosher) dietary laws are kept by many Orthodox Jews; halal food laws determine what is lawful or permitted in Islam; many Hindus are vegetarian in respect of beliefs about ahimsa (non-violence).

Example activities

- Exploring Hanukkah with younger children – taste potato latkes and talk about why food cooked in oil is a good way of remembering the story of Hanukkah.
- Exploring Easter with younger children – ask them to look closely at a hot cross bun. What do they see on it? What might it mean? When do people traditionally eat these?
- Exploring Sikhism – make and taste some karah prasad and explore the significance of giving and sharing food as a sign of welcome and equality.
- Make a class or school cookbook including favourite recipes from a range of religions. This could then be sold as a fundraising exercise and the proceeds given to a charity which is seeking to alleviate hunger in the world.

REtoday
Services

A to Z

Listening

Listening is not only an essential skill in everyday life, it is also an important aspect of spirituality. When active listening takes place individuals are able to close off distracting thoughts and images, give their full attention to their subject, and, as a result, are able to 'hear' and understand at a much more profound level. Developing this 'inner listening' ability is central to spiritual development.

Back to back: an activity to develop 'active listening' skills

Active listening is an important skill, essential if pupils are to participate fully in a variety of RE speaking and listening activities ranging from 'Why do they do that?' – discussions of photographs of worship distributed among 6-year-olds – to structured debates about the sanctity of life with 16-year-olds.

- Sit pupils in pairs back to back, and ask one to describe, and the other to draw, an object, artefact or picture. This focuses sharply on the listening skills of the person drawing the picture, and requires a very active ear.

- Alternatively use this strategy to simulate a telephone conversation, for instance for older pupils someone phoning a helpline with a particular moral dilemma to consider. The role of 'telephone counsellor', well done, is one of the most active listening roles in the world!

- **Follow-up discussion:** What difficulties did you have? Were there any misunderstandings? What caused them? In what ways is this like communicating in ordinary life?

Stilling: an activity to develop 'inner listening' skills

Useful for: fostering empathy and deeper self-awareness; enabling pupils to discover their own inner experience and, as a result, become more able to respect it in others; developing understanding of the value of prayer and meditation within religion.

By experiencing 'stilling', pupils can become aware of their own inner experience and learn to value this aspect of their being.

See also: Stilling.

Masks

Useful for: engaging interest; retelling faith stories; interpretation and visual expression of characteristics such as good and evil.

In south-east Asia, the Hindu epic story of the Ramayana is acted out by travelling theatre groups using traditional costumes and masks.

For example... Masks could be created in art or after-school enrichment activities and used in RE to act out the Ramayana story at Divali. Happy and sad masks to show Peter's changing emotions during Holy Week.

Mental maps

Useful for: planning; making connections between learning; identifying existing ideas at the start of an activity; adding new ideas as they occur during an activity; reviewing learning at the end of a unit; particularly good for visual and logical-mathematical learners.

Mental or mind maps are a visual way for recording the big picture. They work like the brain. We don't think in straight lines – our thoughts shoot off in different directions – just like branches from a trunk. Tony Buzan developed the idea of mind mapping as a visual way of organising and remembering thoughts and information. It works in the way brain patterns do. Whilst not an 'active' learning strategy in itself, it is a 'cognitively active' strategy which, when done as a whole class, draws on the ideas and earlier learning of everyone in the group.

The following activity can be done individually or as a whole class.

- Start with the key word or main idea. Write it at the centre of a large sheet or on the whiteboard.
- Put down all the ideas that come into your head, in any order, but draw lines connecting each thought to another like branches on a tree. It's OK to add new branches and 'twigs' as your mind leaps about – that's the way it works!
- Take each theme or new thought as far as you want to or can.
- Use colours, shapes and symbols to highlight important ideas.

For example... Using a mind map to introduce a topic on Christian and Hindu scriptures

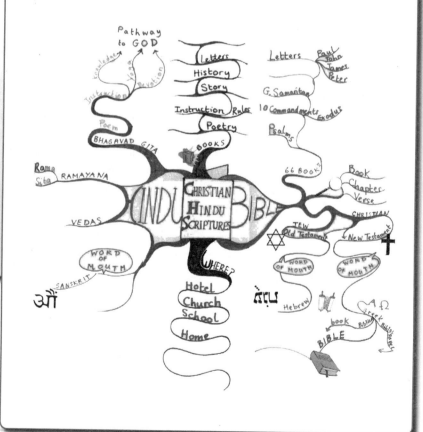

REtoday
Services

A to Z

Mime

Mime is one of the simplest of dramatic arts but can also be one of the most demanding, which makes it suitable for use with all age-groups.

Pupils, working in pairs or small groups, devise a mime to represent the outward expression of an inner feeling (anger, sympathy) or moral virtue (goodness, generosity, compassion). Younger children could mime the feelings of characters in faith stories. Feelings are expressed through movement of the body and expressions on the face.

The process of working out the mime focuses the attention of the pupil, requires empathy and reflection, and helps to raise awareness of the power of inner feelings.

Some tips for using mime

- Make the movements slightly larger than life.
- For younger children, suggest that they follow your lead to start off with – but feel free to improvise their own actions.
- Older pupils can reflect more on what they are doing. Pupils could identify a key moment in a story, mime the experience to others, see if they can guess the moment, and discuss what was happening, why it is significant, was it a 'turning point' in some way?.

For example... an activity for younger primary pupils: miming the Zacchaeus story

Zacchaeus was a little man, but he tried to look bigger by walking around on tiptoe. **(All tiptoe around)**

He was a greedy man who collected money for the Romans. **(Counting money)**

People didn't like him and tried to pretend he wasn't there! **(Head down, arms over face)**

He heard about Jesus and really wanted to see him, so he ran down the street. **(Running on the spot)**

Because he was little he couldn't see over people's heads. So he climbed a tree. **(Arm over arm)**

Suddenly he heard Jesus call him. **(Hand to ear, surprised look)**

Jesus said to him, 'Come down!' and he did. **(Climb down, arm over arm)**

Jesus wanted to have dinner with him, so Zacchaeus led the way. **(Surprise; pointing, leading the way)**

Other people grumbled. **(Angry looks, finger pointing in condemnation)**

Zacchaeus was very happy. **(Face or bodily movements to express joy and delight)**

He poured out his money on the table. **(Take out imaginary purse, open it, tip it out, spread out money)**

'I'll give back everything to all the people.' **(Arms spread wide, facial expression showing he was sorry)**

Music and sounds

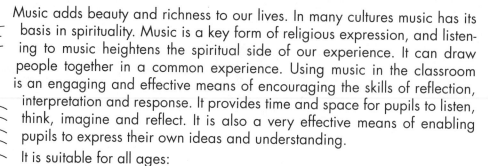

Music adds beauty and richness to our lives. In many cultures music has its basis in spirituality. Music is a key form of religious expression, and listening to music heightens the spiritual side of our experience. It can draw people together in a common experience. Using music in the classroom is an engaging and effective means of encouraging the skills of reflection, interpretation and response. It provides time and space for pupils to listen, think, imagine and reflect. It is also a very effective means of enabling pupils to express their own ideas and understanding.

It is suitable for all ages:

• Catchy action songs retelling faith stories never fail to stimulate and interest young children.

• Older pupils can listen and interpret meaning from contemporary and classical music expressing spiritual or moral experiences; explore how the Muslim call to prayer, the bells in the Hindu arti ceremony or the kirtan (hymn singing with harmonium and tablas) in the Sikh gurdwara are used in worship and what they mean for believers; express insights through writing and performing lyrics using different genres of music.

Using contemporary music

• Do not try to be 'with it' concerning current musical tastes unless you really are. Ask the pupils to name current songs which raise the issues you want to discuss and to bring in their CDs – but listen to them yourself before using them.

• When using contemporary songs try to provide a lyric sheet, perhaps invite pupils to draw as they listen, or give them something visual to focus on whilst listening. Follow-up activities could include:

• Conversation and discussion, using prompt questions such as, 'What do you think the composer was feeling when he wrote this song?' and 'What is the main message of the song? What are your thoughts about this?'

• Poetry, song lyrics or artwork: choose one key idea or line from the song and design a CD cover or T shirt logo and image, or write a poem to express it.

• Older pupils could select music to accompany a *PowerPoint* presentation on an RE theme – love, peace, suffering, joy, celebration.

• When exploring Christian worship, listen to different types of contemporary Christian music, for example from Taizé chants (Gregorian in origin with repetition); Christian pop music; modern hymns of Graham Kendrick. Pupils could identify which groups of people might prefer each and why. Hear what Christians say about how music helps them worship. Listen to clips of contemporary Christian music on the web (e.g. www.threeleggedmusic.com/contemporary.htm).

• When introducing how religions use metaphor for describing God, try using Simon and Garfunkel's 'El Condor Pasa' ('I'd rather be a hammer than a nail'). Ask pupils to consider: 'Would you rather be: a hammer or a nail; a flute or a drum; velvet or cotton; a street or a forest; a sword or a plough? Go on to explore the ways God is described – a mighty rushing wind, a good shepherd, etc.

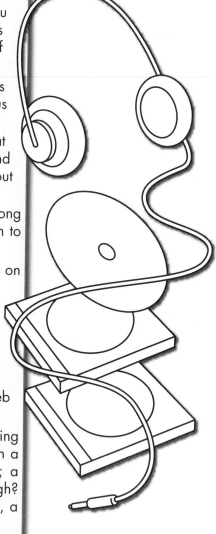

REtoday Services

A to Z

Using classical music

- Set the atmosphere for reflection by playing an appropriate track of quiet music, such as Pachelbel's *Canon* or Satie's *Gymnopedie No 1*.

- When studying biblical themes, listen to how the great composers expressed these ideas. For example, the 'Hallelujah Chorus' from Handel's *Messiah*. Handel told friends that he was inspired by God to write the Hallelujah Chorus. When it was first played the king stood up. To this day people do this when it is played. Pupils could listen and reflect on what they thought God was saying to Handel through the music he wrote. This could lead to discussion of other ways people believe God speaks to them.

Making music

- Primary pupils could use percussion instruments to express their understanding of the symbolism of the Seder plate. One pupil chose a triangle to represent tears dropping to illustrate the salt water. Another beat a drum rapidly to show that the Israelites were in a hurry and did not have time for the bread to rise (matzot).

- Pupils could make up a song to retell a faith story and sing it to a familiar tune.

- Pupils could write and perform a rap on a spiritual or moral theme.

- Borrow some traditional instruments, such as Sikh harmonium and tablas, and make some music linked to work on worship in faith communities.

Using sounds and audio

- Younger primary pupils might use percussion instruments to provide a 'soundtrack' to a faith story read or told by the teacher. For example, in a retelling of the story of Moses in the bulrushes (the Bible, Exodus 2), pupils could make stamping sounds every time Egyptian soldiers are mentioned, tinkling sounds for the water of the Nile, bird and animal sounds for life in the bulrushes, a finger to the lips and appropriate sounds for Miriam (Moses' sister watching over him), a baby sound for Moses and another sound for the princess. Pupils enjoy taking part and have to listen attentively.

- Use sound files from websites and audio tapes to listen to extracts from famous speeches such as Martin Luther King's, reports of news events, and debates about controversial issues such as cloning or genetic engineering. The BBC Religion and Ethics website is a good one (www.bbc.co.uk/religion).

- **'Reporting on local radio'** Pupils could role-play a local radio production team to produce a report on religion in the local community. **See also:** News bulletins.

- Use the *Countdown* clock soundtrack to mark the end of short timed activities.

Mysteries

Useful for: sorting relevant from irrelevant information; interpreting information; making links between disparate bits of information; speculating to form hypotheses; checking, refining and explaining; getting pupils talking about their actual learning and thinking processes.

Pupils are given a central question to answer or a problem to solve, e.g. Why did ... happen? They are then given clues which they have to sort through, make sense of, agree on and produce a plausible (not absolute) answer.

- It is useful to provide information in a way that can be juggled around, such as statements on card. Moving these around and changing their minds is part of the thinking process. It is useful to put these cut-up statements into envelopes for each group with the key question on the front. Try to provide some additional visual clues to the mystery – maps, photographs, diagrams, etc.

- Make sure pupils understand that it is the quality of thinking which matters and that there are not necessarily 'right' answers – just some more or less plausible ones.

- Ask pupils to feed back their answer to the class with a full explanation.

- It is important to spend time afterwards discussing how they actually did the activity. This helps pupils become explicitly aware of problem-solving strategies which can be more widely applied. Prompt questions such as 'What did you do with the cards first?' and 'Why?' will get the discussion started.

Successful 'mystery' activities:

- have a strong 'narrative thread', which helps to get pupils of all abilities interested;

- contain information which sets the place, time and context of the event;

- include some 'red herrings' to make pupils sift information and weigh up relevance;

- do not give all the answers – but make pupils work some things out for themselves.

For example... Try the activity on the next page, 'Why does Gurpal want to take Amrit?', when exploring rites of passage with older primary or younger secondary pupils. This particular activity relates to Sikhism, but could easily be adapted to help pupils explore confirmation or adult baptism in Christianity, Bar or Bat Mitzvah in Judaism; or the sacred thread ceremony in Hinduism.

It's a mystery...
Why does Gurpal want to take Amrit?

Background information

Gurpal is a Sikh and is 13 years old.

His parents are both Khalsa Sikhs.

Gurpal wants to take part in the Amrit ceremony at Baisakhi next year.

Mystery cards

Gurpal goes to the gurdwara on a Sunday.	He is learning Punjabi.	He likes music and is learning to play the tabla.	His favourite subjects at school are History and Maths.
He has an elder sister and a younger brother.	He visited the Harimandir in Amritsar for the first time last year.	Gurpal likes to help in the langar – he usually does his turn when his father does.	Gurpal plays football for the school and for his gurdwara.
One of Gurpal's best friends, Surjit, had his hair cut short last year.	Gurpal has a friend called Jonathan who is Jewish. Jonathan had his Bar Mitzvah recently.	His grandad died a few months ago and Grandma has now come to live with Gurpal's family.	He finds listening to the words of the Guru Granth Sahib during worship very calming.
He wants to be a social worker when he grows up – he thinks this is a good job for a Sikh to do.	He recites prayers from his gutka in the morning before going to school.	Gurpal wants to show he is following the teachings of the Gurus.	He respects all the Gurus and has grown up listening to stories about them.
He takes part in a discussion group for young people at the local gurdwara.	Gurpal believes in God.	He regularly e-mails his cousin who lives in the Punjab.	Gurpal believes that he is ready to take on the responsibilities of being a Khalsa Sikh.

News boards

Useful for: encouraging a sense of self-worth and the valuing of others; enabling pupils within a group (tutor group or primary school class) to share personal experiences, whilst encouraging others to be sensitive and appreciative towards the thoughts, feelings and values of others.

Pupils are invited to place on the news board items of personal interest or concern. Discussion around the area or issue raised can take place.

Variation: A news board can be changed into a questions board and pupils encouraged to put on it any questions they have relating to the topic they are studying. Other pupils might like to try to answer them.

News bulletins

Useful for: consolidating pupil learning from a lesson or series of lessons.

Small groups prepare a one-minute radio news bulletin on the lesson topic. The group elects a 'newsreader'. Each bulletin has 60 seconds only, and bulletins follow in quick succession.

Observation

Giving attention is at the heart of spirituality. Developing the ability to 'see' with insight, awareness and appreciation is a key dimension of spiritual development. Providing pupils with opportunities for long, slow looking encourages reflection and helps pupils to 'see' in a different way, developing spiritual awareness. The example activity below would fit well into RE lessons exploring creation, 'Who am I?', or human nature.

For example... Close inspection

Ask pupils to observe closely their own hands (or face or eyes in a mirror, or a partner's eyes). Compare fingerprints, line patterns on the palm of the hand, the shades of colour and shape in different people's eyes. Consider how each person is unique and special. Pupils could consider what they like and don't like about themselves, what they can and cannot change, what they're good at, what skills they can do with their hands, how their hands can help others.

Also close observation of nature such as minibeasts, spiders' webs, plants or tree bark from the school grounds – or frost, icicles, ice or snow.

Talk about:

* what pupils have noticed for the first time;
* what their careful looking made them think about;
* what they felt.

Give pupils the opportunity to record these sights, thoughts and feelings creatively in words or drawings.

See also: Artefacts – natural objects.

OHP (overhead projector)

There are various ways that this useful piece of equipment can involve pupils in their learning. For example:

- **Jigsaw** Cover up a transparency of a scene from a faith story or an image of an artefact with numbered jigsaw pieces and reveal a piece at a time, asking children to guess what the picture is and/or what they know about it. This is a good activity for identifying earlier learning or drawing together learning at the end of a session. **See also:** Jigsaw.

- Use it for shadow puppetry (see below), for recording children's comments and responses, for creating on-the-spot poems or prayers, or to project an image which acts as a focus for the lesson. Some commercial resources feature OHTs in their packs; alternatively, images can be printed from the internet or photocopied onto transparencies.

Divali shadow puppets – an activity for pupils based on traditional ways of retelling the Ramayana story

In south-east Asia the epic story of the Ramayana is acted out by travelling theatre groups using traditional costumes and masks. Another traditional way of retelling the story uses shadow puppets.

Show pupils examples of silhouettes of the main characters in the story – Rama, Sita, Lakshman, Ravanna, King Dasratha, Queen Kaikeyi, Hanuman.

Give pupils a segment of the story of Rama Sita.

Pupils could then:

- pick one character and make a silhouette drawing of them (modelling it on traditional designs);
- fasten the silhouette securely to a wooden skewer with tape;
- design a setting for the story, drawing it on to an OHT transparency sheet using OHT pens;
- retell the story of the Ramayana, using the silhouettes as shadow puppets against the backdrop setting on OHT screen.

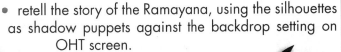

One rule, and we broke it

Useful for: testing out human nature, using the findings as a fun starter to discussion on human perversity, perhaps linked to the Adam and Eve story in Genesis 3; potentially stimulating discussion about human nature and evil.

Set this up with a small group of pupils.

Place a chair in the school entrance hall, or by the dinner queue, in an unusual and prominent place, with a large notice on it saying 'Rule 1. Do not touch this chair'. Leave it during break or lunch time. Some pupils can watch discreetly what happens, and make a tally chart of how many passers-by read the notice, and deliberately touch the chair (including staff).

P

Paper and pen

This is a variation on brainstorming but is more suitable for personally sensitive issues which individuals may not wish to share publicly.

For example... My greatest fear

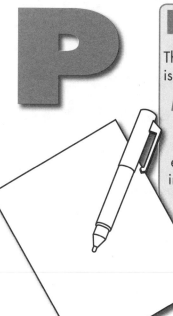

Give out paper and pens. Ask everyone to write down the headings: This Lesson; School; Life in General. Ask them privately to write down their greatest fear or worry concerning each. Ask them to fold these up and place them into a container passed around by the teacher. These can then be read out (being careful to ensure anonymity). Commonly held worries and fears will be identified. Pupils go into groups, each group to be given one fear or worry which is shared by many. Groups suggest three things a person with this fear or worry could do.

Paper chain

Pupils write their own thoughts on small lengths of sticky-backed paper which are then made into loops and joined together to form a chain, which is displayed.

For example...

A prayer chain Pupils write their own prayers or poems relating to a lesson focus.

A chain of hope Pupils write their hopes for the world.

The chain of life As part of a study of the wholeness and interdependence of creation, pupils choose one of the vital elements for human life – for example, fire, light, air, water, soil, plants, living creatures (humans and animals) – and express their thoughts about the value of this element. These are then linked together to form a complete circle. Pupils are asked to talk about what happens if one element or one link in the chain is damaged. Who or what might 'break the chain'? Why? How can we prevent this?

Values chain Pupils write about one key value that they believe is vital for a happy and fulfilled life lived together in community.

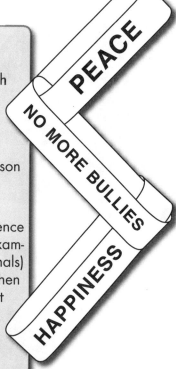

REtoday
Services

Ato**Z**

Photoboard

Useful for: a stimulus for discussion of issues and the exploration of moral decision-making. The completed photoboard impacts on other individuals and classes through display.

This is the telling of a story using a sequence of photographs or images taken from magazines or websites, with dialogue superimposed in speech bubbles. Pupils are asked to produce a short narrative which raises a moral dilemma.

See also: *Dilemmas and Decisions* (RE Today Services) offers forty-eight situations which pose moral dilemmas. These could be used as starting points.

Photographs and pictures

Useful for: encouraging pupils to look carefully, analyse, reflect and interpret the meaning and significance of the images.

Get 'inside' a photograph or picture by 'interrogating' it – asking questions of those in the picture, exploring actions, motives, relationships and so on.

When looking at a picture of an event, ask questions like:

- What can you see in the picture?
- What are the people doing?
- What might they be saying?
- Have you seen anything like this before?
- Can you see all the people who have shared in planning or running this event, or are some of them outside the picture?
- What would happen if one person in this group suddenly stopped taking part?
- How do you think each person is feeling? Have you ever felt like that?

The actual questions will naturally vary depending on the subject matter.

For example... With younger pupils, use Christmas cards with specifically Christian images. Cut up and stick the pictures onto a sheet to form a design. Pupils then write questions around these for others to answer.

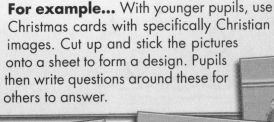

Poetry

The reading and writing of poetry exercises the imagination and helps articulate ideas and feelings which cannot easily be expressed in any other way. A poem was once described as 'an ice-axe to break open the ice-block of our soul'. The following simple structures can be used to encourage pupils to reflect on ideas and express their inner thoughts and feelings. This activity uses literacy skills to express spiritual and religious understanding. Whilst not a physically active strategy, it's a good structure for stimulating cognitive activity!

Some examples of poem structures and activities follow:

Acrostic

A poem which is organised by the initial letters of a key word, either at the beginning of lines, or with lines arranged around them. Make acrostic poems on key RE terms such as belief, spiritual, religious, commitment. Encourage pupils to aim to express the deeper meaning of these words.

C arpenter   Ena**b**ling

H ero   **e**mpowering

R ebel   I**ll**uminating

I nspiring   **L**ife-enhancing

S piritual   Giv**e**s direction

T eacher   **f**aith

Calligram

This is a poem in which the calligraphy, the formation of the letters or the font selected, represents an aspect of the poem's subject. A poem about fear might be written in shaky letters to represent trembling.

(See examples on this page.)

Sonnet

For older pupils (especially those studying Shakespeare), try using sonnets. Have a word with your English specialist if you are not sure.

Sonnets have fourteen lines with ten syllables per line which should have the rhythm ti-tum ti-tum ti-tum ti-tum ti-tum (that is, with the emphasis on the second, fourth, sixth, eighth and tenth syllables). A number of different rhyming patterns were used by classical poets like Milton and Shakespeare, but the simplest to adopt is a-b-a-b, c-d-c-d, e-f-e-f, g-g with the final rhyming couplet delivering a 'punchline'.

Encourage upper secondary pupils to reflect on human beliefs, values and qualities, or moral issues such as human rights, using this structure. They will amaze you with what they can do given the opportunity.

REtoday
Services

AtoZ

Cinquain

This is a five-line poem with a total of twenty-two syllables in the sequence two, four, six, eight, two.

Line 1 – a noun.
Line 2 – two adjectives that agree with the noun.
Line 3 – three verbs.
Line 4 – a short phrase of four words.
Line 5 – a synonym to the first noun.

For example...

To encourage reflection on the term 'lion' as a metaphor for God (Bhagavad Gita) or Sikh use of the term Singh (lion) for male members of the Sikh Khalsa, pupils could devise a cinquain using the above pattern (see the example on this page).

Lion
Strong, powerful.
To roar, to scare, to survive.
Hunts down its prey.
King.

Those who close their minds
To wonder and delight are
Blinder than the blind.

Septain

This is a seven-line poem in the same form as a cinquain (one word – two words – three words – four words – three words – two words – one word).

Haiku

The haiku is a three-line poetic form originating in Japan. The traditional form is five syllables (not words), followed by seven, followed by five. In the first two lines you present your idea and in the third line you should have some type of surprising connection to conclude the poem. The poem captures a moment of awareness or insight and should be written spontaneously to capture the essence of the experience. Haiku does not have any rhyme.

Concrete or shape poems

These are poems in which the layout of the words represents an aspect of the subject. In some cases, these poems are presented as sculptures. Concrete poems blur the distinction between visual and linguistic art, as do other shape poems.

For example...

After looking at examples of prayers, pupils could write their own prayer or poem to express something which matters to them. They could choose a favourite object; if they are writing prayers, a religious object that relates to their own personal faith would be appropriate. They then write their poem or prayer in its shape. These could be decorated with colours and designs appropriate to the content and made into a class prayer book.

See also: Senses poetry.

See also: Senses poetry

'Post-its'

Useful for: getting everyone involved; stimulating reflection and empathy; consolidating learning.

Use these to record pupils' responses – words or phrases – to a piece of narrative, a picture, a story or a video, asking them to put themselves in the place of the person, imagining what the person feels or is thinking in that situation.

For example...

Exploring temptation Telling the story of Ibrahim being tempted by Shaytan to rebel against God; exploring how Muslims express their rejection of evil by stoning the pillars during Hajj. Similar responses may be grouped, pupils sticking their word or phrase in the appropriate section of a large sheet of paper.

Looking at a picture Ask pupils to write their comments and questions and place around a picture.

Drawing together learning Pupils create a simple slogan and an illustration on a 'post-it' to express what they have learned from the lesson or unit of work. These can then be stuck on a large sheet of paper and displayed.

Puppets

Useful for: helping younger pupils retell faith stories; engaging interest; as a distancing tool for pupils to express feelings; enabling the teacher to observe and analyse pupils' learning.

Younger children love stories told using puppets. It can involve the whole group. Some like operating puppets; some like to tell or read the story; some like making a background scene against which a puppet show can be performed.

Puppets don't have to be complicated or expensive. Some simple ways of making your own...

Stick puppets Draw a face on stiff card, cut out and attach to a wooden stick or ruler. These can be silhouettes, and used for shadow puppetry (see 'Overhead Projector').

Paper bag puppets Use a bag 30cm x 15cm. Children draw faces, hair and clothes in strong bright colours. A 'head' could be made by stuffing the corner with crumpled paper and securing with an elastic band.

Glove puppets Cut out a simple shape from some strong fabric, to fit the hand of a child. Machine around the edge and turn inside out. Make a face with fabric pens or other materials.

Finger puppets Draw a face on a piece of paper. Make into a cylinder shape and secure with sellotape.

Questioning

Questioning is a key RE skill. Setting tasks which encourage pupils to ask and respond to deeper questions is the bread and butter of the subject. Understandably, teachers can be concerned about opening up questions that they find difficult to respond to.

Community of enquiry

Useful for: building pupils' skills in asking questions and identifying what an appropriate question might be in a range of contexts; encouraging reflection and 'deeper' thinking skills.

This strategy depends upon pupils listening to a story or narrative, or looking at a picture or watching a video, asking questions about what they see or hear, and then deciding together which questions are the most interesting to discuss as a class. Pupils then discuss without any direct input from the teacher. This takes practice and guidance – but don't give up, it's worth it in the end! This approach originates in the 'philosophy for children' methodology developed by Matthew Lipman.

For example... **Exploring a story from the childhood of Krishna with primary pupils**

- The class listens to the stories of Krishna's childhood, such as Krishna stealing the butter or the story in which his mother sees the whole universe inside his mouth.

- Pupils think of questions they would like to ask, e.g. 'Why was Krishna so silly as to eat dirt when he was supposed to be God? What is the greatest power a god can have?' The questions are recorded on the whiteboard or OHP.

- In pairs or groups, pupils choose one question they wish to explore.

- The teacher scribes the selected questions on the board. These are then sorted out. Through discussion pupils work out which are the more interesting questions and recognise that not all questions have a set answer on which everyone will agree. A class vote decides which question is selected.

- The question is discussed. To start this off, the pupils who proposed the question explain their thoughts. The rest of the class are then encouraged to join in. It is helpful if pupils are given a structure such as 'I agree with...because...' or, 'I disagree with... because...'

(See *REtoday*, summer 2003, page 4 for a fuller account of this activity.)

See also: Ultimate questions; Hotseat.

Probing questions

Useful for: enhancing linguistic competence and critical thinking skills.

Get pupils thinking with challenging questions such as:

- What would the world be like if nothing died?

- What's the largest number you can think of? Now add one!

- If the world started with gases coming together to make a big bang – who or what made the gases?

- What is a good human being? What do you mean by 'good'?

Question box

Each pupil prepares a question on a subject. All the questions are then collected into a box and redistributed to other pupils for them to discover the answer.

For example...

For 7-year-olds All the questions that you can think of about what makes a hero, or what you would ask Jesus, Muhammad ﷺ or Moses if you could.

For 10-year-olds Questions you would like to ask someone featured in a video clip (e.g. a Hindu worshipping at a home shrine); or questions you would ask God if you could; or, what puzzles you about life and death?

For 13-year-olds Questions about what happens when you die, or why there is suffering.

For 16-year-olds Questions about sex ethics, or what you would ask the devil (if there is one).

Ranking

Useful for: sorting, prioritising values and opinions, negotiating, speaking and listening skills, developing evaluation skills.

Ranking involves groups discussing and prioritising statements.

- Pupils are given nine statements on cards. These may be responses to a particular question or viewpoints on an issue.
- Working in groups or pairs pupils sort the cards, putting the one they agree with most at the top, the one they agree with least at the bottom, and the others between to form a diamond shape:

Strongly agree

Agree

Disagree

Strongly disagree

For example... Why is the Bible such a bestseller?

People are given Bibles as presents – schoolchildren, prisoners, hotels – that's why so many are sold.	The Bible helps people at times of need – they find it comforting.	The Bible is full of famous stories – that's why people love it.
Christians believe that God speaks to people through the Bible.	Some people read the Bible every day as a religious duty.	The Bible answers puzzling questions about such things as what happens when we die – people want to know these things.
The Bible has wisdom, prayers and guidance for life – that's why Christians use it so much.	The Bible explains how God loves everyone – it makes people feel special.	Some people have a Bible on the shelf but don't really read it.

Variations: It doesn't always have to be agree/disagree. Pupils could be asked to rank people's actions and responses to a situation on the basis of most to least surprising. Ranking can also be used to sort and prioritise activities in a group work activity or items for discussion on an agenda.

See also: Games.

Re-enactment

Useful for: getting inside a religious story; developing empathy; speaking and listening skills.

A known event is re-enacted exactly to try to access its dynamics, relationships, meanings and so on. The better the briefing, the better the results. This activity can be effectively used with religious story, but take care to avoid offending some faith traditions by casting God, and Muhammad ﷺ in the case of Islam. Draw out the deeper meaning of the story by using carefully planned probing questions.

See also: Drama activities.

Reflection

Reflection is a key skill, central to Religious Education. In RE, it involves:

- pondering on feelings, relationships and experiences, beliefs, practices and lifestyles;
- thinking and speaking carefully about questions about life and its meaning (sometimes called ultimate questions).

Carefully planned activities will enable pupils to....

- take time to stand back and think over aspects of experience such as feelings, actions, relationships, new ideas, beliefs and practices;
- value stillness and silence as an aid to reflection;
- use their imagination to enter into experiences;
- make connections with their own lives.

Reflective activities

For this kind of activity, a good working relationship, based on trust and consideration of the needs of others is important. Pupils should be seated comfortably in an atmosphere conducive to reflective thinking, using appropriate lighting, music, and so on. The leader introduces the contemplative activity through words or visual stimuli. The reflective activity is followed up in one of a number of ways, allowing pupils to express and explore their insights and feelings. Reflections can be expressed through a variety of media including art, music and poetry as well as prose.

PLEASE DO NOT DISTURB

Preparing for reflection: stilling

An activity which literally 'stills' or calms the body and mind. It is most often used as a way in to a variety of activities which help pupils acknowledge and explore the spiritual dimension of life. By experiencing 'stilling' and 'inner listening' pupils can become aware of their own inner experience and learn to value this aspect of their being. It is only when we discover our inner experience that we are able to respect it in other people.

A stilling activity usually involves;

- relaxation (releasing tensions);
- attentive listening;
- focusing on an object or taking part in a visualisation activity;
- expressing personal ideas and insights (often in a creative way);
- sharing ideas (with no obligation to join in).

Linked with guided visualisation, stilling is extremely effective and powerful, but there are ground rules and if you have never used this strategy with a class or group before you need to be careful and not expect too much.

Some tips

- Negotiate some ground rules with pupils. These may include: respecting the silence, feelings, space of others; being allowed to 'opt out' at any stage but agreeing not to disturb others; staying silent at the end of the activity.
- Put a note on the door to avoid disturbances, and tell colleagues what you are doing.
- Rearrange seating to make it more conducive to the activity. Sit on chairs, not on the floor.
- Use stilling as a preparation for a further activity such as guided visualisation.

Stilling script

I'd like to invite you to take part in a short reflective activity.

Before we begin we will spend a few moments settling ourselves down. After this, I will ask you to listen carefully and imagine yourselves in the scene I will describe to you.

Remember that times of quiet reflection can be very special. I would ask each of you to respect everyone's right to quiet to enjoy this activity.

You may like to close your eyes or focus on a spot on the ground. If you feel uncomfortable in any way with what we are doing, simply remain sitting quietly so that you don't disturb others.

To start off, we are going to do a little exercise to become really still and focused.

Make sure you're sitting in a comfortable position ... sitting upright so that you can breathe easily, feet on the floor, hands resting comfortably in your lap.

Now gently close your eyes or look at a spot on the ground so that you are not distracted.

Listen carefully: what can you hear outside the room ... sounds which have been here all the time but which you may not have noticed before. (Pause)

Now focus your mind on sounds in this room ... what can you hear? (Pause)

Now I'd like you to listen to a unique sound ... the sound of your own breathing. Listen carefully to your own breath, as it flows in and out of your body. Let any tensions and anxieties flow out with your outward breath.

Now I'd like you to listen as I take you on an imaginary journey...

(Guided visualisation activity follows.)

Some reflective activities

Guided visualisation

This is the use of imagination to enter into a story. The teacher leads pupils through a story sequence told in the present tense; the pupil takes an active role in the story.

See also: Guided visualisation.

Reflection circles

Pupils take it in turns to share their thoughts on a question or idea. The teacher seeks to provide a supportive and accepting atmosphere and takes part in all the activities. A number of activities and approaches can be used, including icebreakers, sentence starters, discussion starters, sharing views and opinions.

Circle time, structured time when the class gathers to speak, listen, share concerns and issues, is increasingly being used in many primary and in some secondary schools as part of class or tutor time or as an element in a personal and social education programme.

Reflection circles are also used as plenary activities at the end of a session to allow and encourage reflection on what has been learned and how. In this context, reflection concerns reviewing learning rather than pondering meaning.

Reflective tasks

Use music, images, artefacts, sound-bites, video clips or human stories to stimulate reflection on questions such as, 'What matters most?', 'Who is in control?', or, 'What is life for?'

Pupils could select images and texts to produce their own *PowerPoint* presentation in response to an ultimate question such as 'Why do people suffer?' or 'Is there life after death?'

See also: Diary of Reflection activity; *Reflections* (edited by Rosemary Rivett, RE Today Services, 2004).

> Reflection differs from evaluation in seeking pupils' personal thoughts without necessarily requiring reference to evidence or argument. The best work was found where these tasks were based clearly on what had been learnt rather than personal reflections without a stimulus.
>
> Barbara Wintersgill HMI
> (*Task setting in RE at Key Stage 3, 2000*)

Role-play

Useful for: arousing interest and active participation; using non-verbal communication skills; helping pupils understand the position and feelings of others, analysing a story or an incident; developing self-confidence.

In role-play, pupils imagine they are in a situation and behave as they would in the role. Pupils are asked to pretend they are one of the people concerned.

It is, however, not an end in itself. Structured reflective and expressive activities need to follow to explore insights stimulated by the role-play.

Getting prepared for role-play

An effective way of ensuring everyone fully understands the role-play scenario and their own role within it is to prepare cards which summarise the situation on one side and provide a role description on the other. Allow time for pupils to familiarise themselves with these and to think themselves 'into role'.

Sample follow-up questions

- What was happening in the role-play?
- How did the pupils feel (in role)?
- What did they feel about each other's actions?
- What did they learn from the role-play?

Example role-play situations

Faith story Getting inside a faith story by asking pupils to identify a key moment or a turning point in the story, identifying the characters, discussing what each would be feeling and doing; role-play the action. Use a digital camera to record key moments. Use ICT to add speech bubbles to express key thoughts and feelings of the characters in the scene.

Interviews and interrogations Roles might include: journalists; detectives; scientists; radio reporters; documentary film crews; jurors; police.

Meetings Simulation of decision-making bodies: parish council meeting; public enquiry; protest meeting; school council; action group.

Overheard conversation Hiding, spying and eavesdropping roles can explore themes like truth and lies, gossip, secrets, and so on. Groups of three can develop overheard conversation.

Witness Taking the role of a participant in an enquiry or trial, each person explains what they saw, heard and knew. This can be useful for exploring religious experience, for example Guru Nanak's disappearance or Paul's conversion.

Variations

Use of 'freeze-frame' (see the relevant section) in the middle of a role-play provides an opportunity for 'thought-tapping'. Pupils speak aloud their private thoughts and reactions 'in role'. The teacher freezes the improvisation and activates an individual by tapping them on the shoulder.

Two role-play activities to help pupils learn about their own learning

Useful for: developing self-awareness as a learner; developing skills for self-assessment and target-setting.

Try asking pupils to put themselves in the role of the examiner or the teacher. Marking and report writing are two such activities. The role-play activities outlined opposite help pupils to see the process 'from the other side' – giving them new insights and a chance to take more responsibility for their own learning and progress in the future.

REtoday Services

A to Z

Writing my own report: a role-play activity for primary and secondary pupils

This activity encourages pupils to reflect on their achievements in RE, identify aspects for improvement and, over time, take more responsibility for their own progress. It takes pupils seriously and recognises that the person who knows most about how they are doing is the pupil him- or herself. It works best when there is an element of choice and a framework of sentence starters to focus pupils' thinking.

RE: writing my own report

- This sheet is to help you write about the work you have been doing in RE.
- Write as much as you can, but do at least ten sentences, choosing starters from five or more boxes.
- Think and write carefully on your own.

• This RE topic has made me think about... • Since doing this work in RE I have changed my mind about... • My opinions are... • I believe... • I can't make my mind up about... • Other people think...	• In RE we have been learning about... • What we've done in RE is... • Our lessons in RE have been about... • In RE I've learned all about... • The main things I did in RE were...	• I could have improved my RE work by... • To do better in RE I will... • If I started this work again I would... • The effort I put in was... • I am most pleased with... • My RE written work is...
• The best bit of the work was... • What I enjoyed about it was... • I found it interesting when... • The good thing about this work was...	• Now I understand more about... • Before doing this work in RE I didn't realise that... • One thing that made me think was... • It's surprising that... • I'm curious to find out more about... • I'm still puzzled about... • I can't be sure that... • One fascinating thing is...	• The advice I would give to someone starting this work would be... • Overall, my work has been... • From this work, I have gained... • Generally, RE has been... • Finally, I would like to say...

You are the examiner: a role-play for GCSE RE students

This simple activity can be used to build up the self-awareness and exam skills of groups of GCSE RE or RS students. It puts them in the role of the examiner, and gets them to notice some common pitfalls of examination writing. It should be followed up by getting students to write the essay themselves. You might even get them to mark the results in pairs. Self-aware students write more, answer more accurately and make the most of their knowledge.

- Give pupils a GCSE examination question and marking guidelines (based on board guidelines).
- Give pupils four specimen answers illustrating different levels of response – keep these to less than one side of A4 if possible.
- Ask pupils to:
  - give each a mark by applying the mark scheme;
  - state, using bullet points, what advice they would give each candidate about how to improve his or her writing in RE exams.
- Follow up with feedback discussion. Ask pupils to record what they need to do in future to improve their own essay writing.

Rucksack

Pupils often carry rucksacks stuffed full of the bits and pieces of daily living. This everyday object can be used as a focus for reflection. The examples here illustrate a way of using it to enable pupils to analyse what matters most to them (values clarification), and a way to encourage empathy with people in need.

What matters most?

Useful for: a starter activity for helping pupils to begin thinking about what matters most.

Imagine that you are going on a long journey (to somewhere hot or cold, isolated or busy, for example). All you can take with you are the things that you can fit into your rucksack – the bare necessities. What would you choose to take and why?

People in need

Useful for: linking with a topic on forgiveness – reflecting on the psychological importance of letting go of grudges and ill feelings towards others.

Imagine that you can put not only things but qualities into your rucksack (kindness, friendship, courage). Think and talk about:

* the qualities you would like to demonstrate or take with you on your journey through life;
* the sorts of things we sometimes carry around with us that we would be better off leaving behind (grudges, regrets and so on).

Refugee

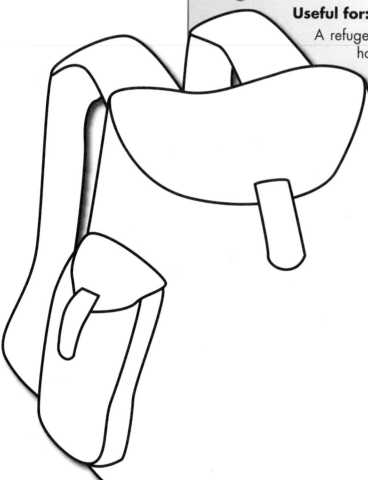

Useful for: developing empathy.

A refugee is a person who is forced to leave his or her home country to escape from danger.

* Imagine you have only 10 minutes to leave your home.
* You can only take a rucksack with you.
* You cannot take any other item which is carried separately.
* You cannot ask anyone else to carry anything for you.
* What will you take? Draw what you will take inside the rucksack outline.
* Which item would you keep if everything else had to be left behind?

REtoday
Services

A to Z

Sensory activities

The more pupils use their senses of touch, hearing, taste, sight and smell, the more they will learn and remember. This is true of all pupils, whatever their ability, and is particularly true for pupils with special educational needs.

Some of the ways this can be developed in Religious Education are indicated in the chart below. Many of the activities are described in this publication. You will be able to add others. Notice our addition of a 'sixth sense'!

Multi-sensory and experiential learning in RE

Sense	Possible RE activities
Sight	**Art work** e.g. pictures; posters; greetings cards **Artefacts** e.g. cross; tallit **Books** **Video, slides or OHT** **Visits** **Websites**, *PowerPoint* presentations or whiteboard displays
Hearing	**Audio prompts** Religious sounds, e.g. Muslim call to prayer; aum **Extracts from soundtracks** e.g. speeches (Martin Luther King) **Listening to stories** e.g. case studies; biography; faith stories **Listening to each other** e.g. active listening; circle activities; discussion groups **Music** e.g. pop song; classical music as aid to reflection; worship music e.g. Sikh kirtan **'Stilling' activities** – Learning to listen with attention
Touch	**Artefacts** (Exploring through feely bags or boxes) **Buildings** e.g. church visit – stone pillars, font, symbols **Drama, role play, mime, freeze-frame** e.g. using hands to express emotions (friendship, anger); religious symbolism e.g. prayer, devotion; freeze-frame key moment in faith story **Making** e.g. model of mosque; Easter garden; games, music **Natural objects** e.g. leaves, stones, shells (Creation) **Playing games** e.g. dreidel game (Jewish Hanukkah)
Taste	**Eating and drinking** Linked to celebration of festivals and holy days, e.g. potato latkes (Hanukkah); Matzot, haroset, salt water, etc. (Pesach); Asian sweets (Diwali); Challah bread (Shabbat/Pesach) **Used in religious ritual and ceremony** e.g. bread and wine (Eucharist); karah prasad (Sikh worship); food shared in the langar (Sikhism)
Smell	**Candles** e.g. an aid to reflection; linked to worship; arti ceremony in Hinduism **Incense** Hindu worship; Roman Catholic or High Anglican worship **Spice box or Havdallah candle** Marking end of Shabbat
Wonder	**Expressing personal responses and insights** e.g. sentence starters: 'Something this makes me think about or want to ask…' **Probing questioning** e.g. 'If you were to ask God one question, what would it be?' **Recording telling statements and questions** e.g. wall of wisdom **Reflective writing** Using prose, e.g. writing a reflective diary, or poetry, e.g. using structures such as cinquains or haiku **Structured reflection opportunities** e.g. prayer activity; guided visualisation

Sensory activity: Guess who or what?

This activity concentrates on the sense of sight (through its absence) and raises awareness of the ability to 'see' through other senses, in this case touch. This can be done in pairs or larger groups. It simply involves a blindfolded person recognising a person or object by touch – as in the TV show *They Think It's All Over*, where panellists have to guess the mystery personality by touch alone.

Sensory activity: Senses poetry

This exercise can be done using any video clip, poster or picture. Imagine you are a bystander at the scene depicted (or one of the characters in it). Write a six-line poem on what you see, hear, touch, taste, smell and wonder (one line for each). This basic format below can be adapted, for example allocating two lines for each sense or concentrating on only two senses. The format can be as simple or as complex as you require, depending on the ages and aptitudes of the pupils involved. Invite pupils to share their poetry with others. They may be reluctant to voice their poetry, but may be willing for their poem to go into a class book.

I saw...	(I noticed...)
I heard...	(I wanted to say...)
I touched...	(I felt...)
I tasted...	(It reminded me of...)
I could smell...	(It was like...)
I wondered...	(It made me think about...)

My idea of heaven is...

Sentence completion

Useful for: reflective thinking; encourages pupils to clarify their thoughts, feelings and opinions and gives them confidence in expressing them. It promotes listening skills.

Many teachers may already use this as a simple means of testing knowledge but its purpose here is different. It is a way of getting pupils to express their own hopes, fears, feelings and self-evaluations. It can be used in a variety of contexts.

For example...

The teacher stimulates a discussion by writing an unfinished sentence on the board and asking pupils to complete it either verbally or in writing. Select pupils to share their ideas – for example, ask the back row or table to read out their responses to the first sentence, another group to the second, another to the third and so on – until all pupils have had the opportunity to be involved.

Starting discussion
- My idea of heaven is...
- My hope for the world is...

Expressing feelings
- I feel (happy) when...

Observation
- I noticed...

Negotiation
- I would like to...

See also: Role-play ('Writing my own report'); Can of Worms.

Similarities and differences

Useful for: making pupils think hard about words and the meaning of ideas; using existing knowledge as a bridge to new understanding; finding out what pupils already know and understand; clarifying thinking within and between religions.

This thinking skills activity draws on a format used in the television programme *Have I Got News for You*, in which several images are shown and participants have to choose the odd one out and give their reasons. The classroom activity involves pupils being given sets of three items and asked to analyse the characteristics which are unique to each, what is shared by each pair, and what is shared by all.

For example...

To introduce religious teaching on evil in the form of Satan or Iblis, pupils are asked to identify two historical characters who personify evil. These may be Hitler, Vlad the Impaler or a similar 'evil' character of their choice. Satan or Iblis makes up the third character. By identifying known characteristics of the fictional characters, pupils are able to reason out some of the characteristics Muslims or Christians attribute to Iblis or Satan. The activity works best when pupils are given a response grid to complete – see the example below.

Other possible sets of three

church – library – mosque
vicar – teacher – rabbi
Muslim – Christian – Jew
heaven – nirvana – coffin
Roman Catholic – Baptist – Quaker
design – accident – evolution
knowing – believing – holding an opinion

You will be able to think of others.

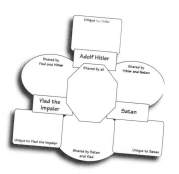

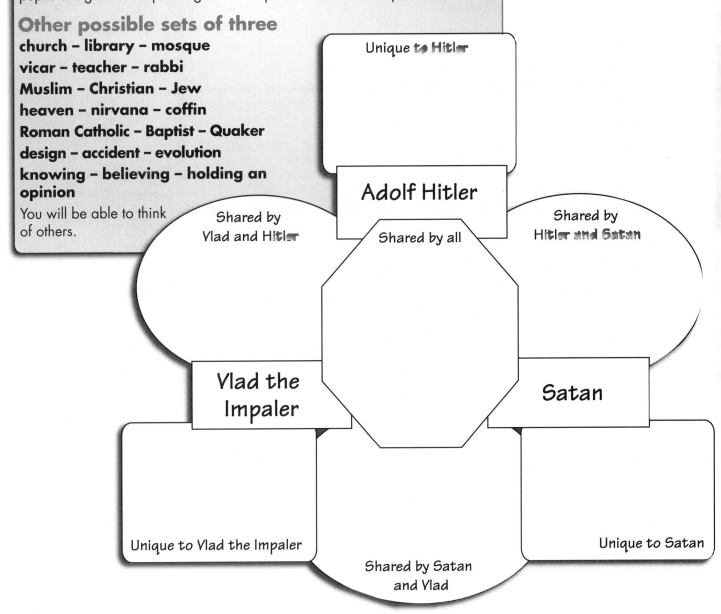

Unique to Hitler

Adolf Hitler

Shared by Vlad and Hitler

Shared by all

Shared by Hitler and Satan

Vlad the Impaler

Satan

Unique to Vlad the Impaler

Shared by Satan and Vlad

Unique to Satan

Story

Stories from faith and secular traditions, from literature, and from contemporary society, if selected carefully and explored sensitively, provide important opportunities for personal and spiritual growth in the classroom. They help us to make sense of our own experience and to gain insights from other people's.

Using stories from faith traditions Remember that many of these stories are from the sacred writings of the faith community involved and as such convey religious and spiritual truths to believers, and consequently are often revered. In Religious Education we are seeking to explore the meaning a story holds for believers and to open up the possibility that it connects with the lives of all pupils, irrespective of their faith or non-faith position.

Ways of telling stories

- **Watch and listen** – use video, audio tapes or teacher as storyteller; or invite a local faith member to tell the story and explain what it means to them.
- **Read** from children's storybooks, the Bible and other sacred texts.
- **Enter into the story imaginatively** (see 'Guided visualisation').
- **Role-play and freeze-frame** the action to find out what characters are thinking and feeling. Photograph and, using ICT, add speech bubbles to images. (See also: 'Role-play' and 'Freeze-frame'.)
- **Mime a story** with appropriate actions (see 'Mime').
- **Use shadow or ordinary puppets** (see 'Puppets' or 'Overhead projector').
- **Use music** to tell the story (see 'Music').
- **'Read'** a painting or a graphic. Work out the story behind a visual scene. (See also: 'Photographs and pictures'.)
- **Make a story box** and play a game (see 'Box story').

Ways of using stories

- Imagine you are a character in the story and write a **diary** entry for the day.
- Write a **poem** expressing the key feelings. (Try using a structure, e.g. haiku or septain, to help pupils).
- Produce drawings, artwork and speech bubbles of different parts of the story for a class **poster**.
- Write the script for a **news** report about the incident and record it as an audio tape.
- Produce a **comic strip** version with pictures and speech bubbles.
- Create a **mime** or a **dance** to express a key moment in the story.
- Tell the story of **what happened next**.
- Write a version of the story for **younger** pupils.
- Write a **letter** from one character to another describing what happened.
- Create a **tape** of the story for younger children.
- Ask, **'What if...?'**
- Go back to key events and **change directions** and outcomes.
- Retell the story from **another person's perspective**.

REtoday
Services

A to Z

Retelling story in RE – activities for 4–7-year-olds

By the age of 7, most pupils should be able to retell religious stories and suggest their meanings. Teachers need to provide a range of structures and activities to help children do this. Some approaches often used are:

- **writing frames and sentence starters** – provides structure;
- **sequencing events in a story using pictures and/or sentences** – helps in ordering, familiarising children with the narrative and the consolidation of learning;
- **producing their own version of the story**, illustrated and perhaps in the form of a zig-zag book or origami book – can give a sense of achievement and develop both written and artistic expression skill;
- **role-play** – encourages empathy and engagement;
- **make a story box and play a game** (see 'Box story').

Making a six-page origami book

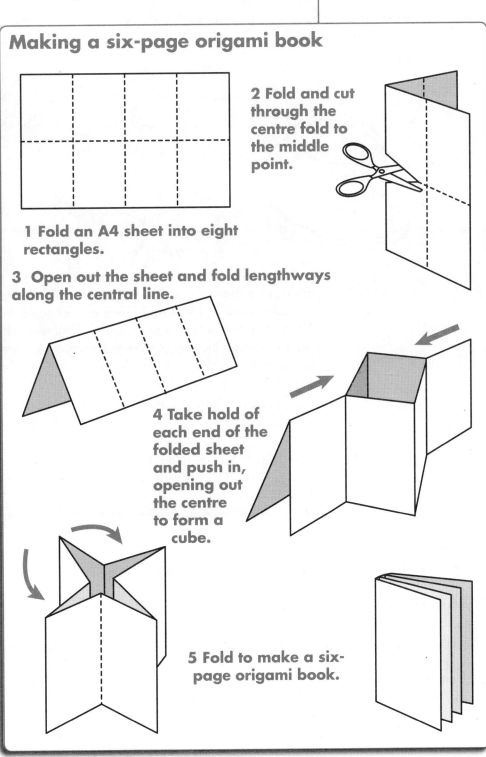

1 Fold an A4 sheet into eight rectangles.

2 Fold and cut through the centre fold to the middle point.

3 Open out the sheet and fold lengthways along the central line.

4 Take hold of each end of the folded sheet and push in, opening out the centre to form a cube.

5 Fold to make a six-page origami book.

Thinking hats

Useful for: encouraging pupils to think and explore problems and issues in a range of different ways and encouraging them to reflect on their own thinking; helping older pupils plan and develop ideas for examination essay writing.

This method, developed by Edward de Bono, is a framework for thinking. There are six imaginary thinking hats, each having a different colour. When you 'put on' a hat, you operate exclusively in that mode of thinking. Each of the six hats represents a different mode of thinking which we all possess – for example, negative, positive, factual, imaginative. The hats are:

White hat
facts; details; questions

What information do we have or need?

Yellow hat
benefits; strengths; advantages

What are the good things?

Black hat
difficulties; weaknesses; dangers

What are the problems?

Red hat
feelings; hunches; intuition

How do we feel about this?

Green hat
suggestions; ideas; alternatives

What other possibilities are there?

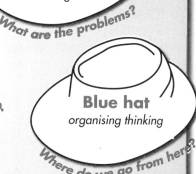

Blue hat
organising thinking

Where do we go from here?

For example...

This strategy can be used to help pupils to explore different interpretations of a story or to collate ideas for an essay. For example, Jesus healing on the Sabbath or the trial and crucifixion of Jesus. Pupils wearing the white hat would give the factual information about the event; others wearing the red hat would focus on the feelings the event evokes in some Christians today; a black hat wearer might outline any questions and problems the story raises; whilst a yellow hat wearer might summarise the value and importance of the event.

Each person or group interprets the meaning or implication of the story differently because each has a different focus for thinking. It works best with short time limits.

See also: *Six Thinking Hats* by Edward de Bono (Penguin Books, ISBN 0140296662; CD version for schools available from www.edwdebono.com/debono/shcd1.htm).

Thought for the day

Useful for: applying religious or philosophical ideas to contemporary situations; developing literacy skills.

Thought for the Day is a two minute reflection on the news from a faith perspective, broadcast daily on Radio 4. It is often witty, contemporary and succinct. Pick out a recent example from the BBC Religion and Ethics website (www.bbc.co.uk/religion/programmes/thought) and listen to the sound file, perhaps following the words at the same time. Most are about 500 words long. More able pupils could write, perform and/or record their own thought for the day.

Transporting a character

Useful for: encouraging analysis of the life and teaching of individuals and application of learning to a new situation; using imagination and speculation.

This is a drama technique in which a character is taken to a different place or time, or to interact with a different set of characters.

For example... Jesus comes to my town

In groups, pupils brainstorm ideas about, 'What if Jesus came to my home town today? What would he say and do? Who would he see and talk to? What would he say? What would he do? What might he look like?' The painting by Antonio Rolls 'Jesus on the Tube' (*Picturing Jesus* pack A, RE Today Services) could provide a stimulus for the activity.

Variations of this might be if Martin Luther King or Mahatma Gandhi visited.

Trust games

Useful for: developing trust and collaboration within the group – essential ingredients to learning in RE, where a 'safe environment' for sharing personal thoughts, beliefs and ideas is necessary.

All of the following need careful preparation and a safe environment (for example, soft mats for landing). The aim is to develop co-operation and confidence in others.

Back to back

In pairs, A and B stand back to back and link through each other's arms. They now have to sit down and stand up together.

Blindfold find

All the members of the group are blindfolded and put in different parts of the room. They have to link up with each other as quickly as possible. This is made more difficult if a 'no talking' rule is imposed.

Sitting circle

A group of people (ten or more) form a circle and then sit   down. If it is done correctly then everyone is supported by everyone else.

Red   **Life**

Orange   **Death**

Yellow Humanity

Green The world

Blue   **Good**

Indigo   **Evil**

Violet   **God**

Ultimate questions

Useful for: getting pupils thinking about the difference between scientific or empirical questions and religious questions, and showing that there are areas of human questioning which science cannot touch.

Prepare strips of coloured paper representing the colours of the rainbow. Each colour represents a different aspect of human experience (see the list on this page). You, or your pupils, may come up with other categories you wish to add.

- Pupils think of as many questions as possible which no one can answer, under each of these headings, and write them on the appropriate coloured strip.

- Mix up all the strips in a container so that questions are not attributable to individuals, and then sort them into their colours.

- Make seven groups, one for each colour. Ask pupils to sift the questions (some of which will be very similar), and reduce them to a manageable number for display while ensuring that these include the questions the pupils think are most important. These are then used to create a 'rainbow' of ultimate questions.

- In groups of four, pupils identify four questions from the 'rainbow' they would want to ask God to answer if they could. Taking responsibility for one question each (but working in pairs), they research what 'answers' members of different faiths might suggest.

- Individual work: pupils select one question and prepare a short presentation explaining why they think it interesting and important, gathering a range of responses to the question.

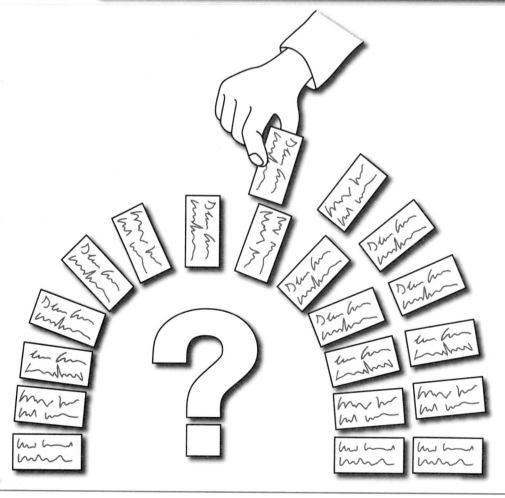

Values

These are various activities which can be employed to help pupils clarify the values which they hold within themselves. (See the index for a full list of other values activities included in this book.)

Select a statement

Place several controversial values statements around the room for the group to choose from. Ask everyone to go and stand next to the statement that they agree with the most. They can then discuss their thoughts and feelings with the people in their area and then with the full group. The aim is to help pupils identify and clarify their values and listen to other opinions. This activity helps develop evaluation skills.

See also: Agree/disagree.

Personal statement

Give every group member four cards and ask them to write down a statement on each card on a particular issue. When this has been completed the cards are collected in and shuffled, then two cards are dealt out to each member. If an individual is satisfied with the statements on the cards, they can be kept. If not, one card may be exchanged at a time by selecting a new one and throwing the old one away face up. As it moves around the group and comes back it can be chosen again, and the game continues until each person is satisfied with the cards they have. At the end, each member must explain and justify the cards kept. This may be done in small groups or as a whole class.

Values auction: personal values

Aim

To engage pupils in a decision-making process which helps them to prioritise their personal values.

Preparation

- Get pupils to create and photocopy a list of values of different sorts. Some examples are given in the margin. (Adapt this list to make it appropriate to the topics under discussion and to keep it up to date).
- Make coloured cards to represent different amounts of money. Each group will need £1000 in mixed cards (e.g. 12 x £50; 12 x £20; 8 x £10; 12 x £5.00; 20 x £1.00).
- Divide the class into groups of up to four people.

Procedure

- Give each group a list of the values and £1000 in mixed cards.
- Give the groups 10 minutes to look through the list of values and decide which are worth most to their lives. When the auction starts they will be asked to bid for the things they value. The highest bidder will receive the item.
- Auction off each item in turn until everything is sold.

Follow-up discussion

- Which items received the most bids, and why?
- Which items received few bids, and why?
- What other things do people in the group value that were not on the list?
- What reasons do people give for their bids? Why do they believe that these are important?
- What kinds of things influence our values? (Consider faith, upbringing, peer pressure, etc.)
- Who decides our values?

Popularity
Good parent
Good health
Friends
Freedom
Good education
Self-discipline
Having fun
Sporting skills
Feeling safe
Honesty
Vegetarianism
Fame
Religious faith
A clean
  environment
Love
A family
Space to be alone
A pet
Enough to eat
A big house
A special talent
Intelligence
Designer clothes
Sight

Visitors

Carefully selected and briefed visitors are an invaluable way to stimulate interest and pupil participation. To generate the right atmosphere and to make the best use of the person's time, both the visitor and the group need to be carefully prepared.

The visitor needs to:

- understand the context of the visit and the amount of time available;
- be told the age and ability of the pupils and the topic they are working on;
- be aware of any important background information he or she needs, especially if dealing with personally sensitive issues;
- discuss with you how they wish to use the session;
- be advised about what to expect in terms of pupil response and participation.

The pupils need to be:

- told who is coming in, when and why;
- briefed on the issues which are to be addressed;
- asked to prepare questions to ask the visitor.

Visitors can be used in the following ways:

- with small groups of pupils, who have the responsibility for preparing an agenda and then the opportunity to practise social skills and learn about the chosen topic;
- with the whole class;
- in a *Question Time* format as a visiting expert prepared to answer questions from the audience.

For further guidance on working with visitors, see *Religious Believers Visiting Schools* (RE Today Services, 2003).

Visitor preparation activity

Useful for: understanding the importance of generating and posing open-ended questions which give the visitor 'space' to explain his or her views; understanding the need for careful listening to hear what the speaker is really saying; sensitivity to appropriate and inappropriate questions, empathising with the visitor's feelings; practising the courtesies of meeting, greeting, introducing, thanking.

- Explain the proposed lesson: interviewing a visitor (for example, youth leader, minister, counsellor, imam).
- Stress the importance of asking questions and listening to answers.
- Ask pupils to think about whether their questions are 'open' or 'loaded' and whether they could be offensive.
- Now get groups of four pupils to generate four sensible questions to put to the visitor.

The teacher must discuss: appropriate questions and ground rules for good behaviour; privacy; open and closed questions. Two or three pupils will be elected or chosen by the teacher to meet, greet, and introduce the visitor. Pupils are also appointed to give a vote of thanks and accompany the visitor to reception. These pupils need to rehearse these functions and jobs.

Wall of wisdom

Useful for: consolidating, celebrating and extending learning; recognising pupils' achievement and insight; building self-esteem; provoking discussion.

A wall display values and records pupils' observations, questions and insights arising from their learning in RE.

	Don't give up on life there is always HOPE		

			Heaven is a world of love	

	People are scared of what they don't know		

Variation

As part of an activity on Christian Aid, borrow an idea from one of their fundraisers. One volunteer cut up empty cereal packets and covered them with paper to make white 'bricks', with which she built a wall to symbolise world hunger. Visitors wrote their own statements, prayers and poems about world poverty and injustice on these bricks. This would make a creative and interesting wall to stimulate further reflection (*Christian Aid News,* spring 2003).

X-files

In pairs, pupils role-play the parts of two 'federal agents', one a believer and the other sceptical about a reported event, for example one of the miracles of Jesus such as the stilling of the storm or the raising of Lazarus. They 'interrogate' their evidence in role.

Y

Yardstick

Useful for: stimulating discussion on a particular moral principle or on the wider issue of whether there are moral absolutes and, if not, how you decide what principle to apply in individual cases.

Pupils are given a statement to act as a 'yardstick' – something to measure everything else by – for example, 'Treat others as you would like to be treated yourself'. Pupils are then given, or devise for themselves, dilemmas or situations in which that yardstick has to be applied.

For example...

Yardstick 'You should always tell your teacher if someone does something wrong.'

Dilemma What would you do if the pupil who has done something wrong is:
- someone you don't like?
- your best friend?
- you?

Yardstick 'It is always wrong to take life.'

Dilemma What would you do if you are:
- in the army and being sent to fight in a war?
- a doctor deciding whether or not to allow a rape victim to have an abortion?
- a man or woman whose wife or husband is being threatened by an armed robber?

Yes or no

Useful for: a plenary or summative activity at the end of a session or unit of work to assess factual knowledge and simple understanding.

Devise a list of questions about a particular topic or belief to which the answer is either yes or no, right or wrong, or true or false.

Variation

In groups of three or four, pupils devise their own questions on an aspect of a given topic or belief which require answers of either yes or no. They then 'test' another group in the class, who, in turn, test them on a different aspect.

For example... On the theme of the Sikh celebration of Baisakhi, groups in the class are given these aspects: the founding of the Khalsa; the life of Guru Gobind Singh; the Amrit ceremony; how Baisakhi is celebrated today.

See also:
Zebra.

Yo-yo

Useful for: encouraging paired or small-group discussion.

One person, A, starts off the discussion by making a brief statement, which the next person, B, 'picks up' and comments on or extends. A then responds to the comment or extension and B responds again and so on, passing the statement back and forth, developing it as they go along.

Variation: Conscience corridor

Useful for: role-playing moral decision-making or facing temptation.

This can be used as plenary to an activity in which an individual is facing a hard decision, such as the younger son in the story of the prodigal son (the Bible, Luke 15). Pupils stand in two rows facing one another. Following role-play, the pupil 'playing' the prodigal son walks down the middle of the corridor listening to advice from both sides. One side says positive, encouraging things such as, 'Your father will forgive you'; the other side puts the opposite point of view: 'Stay away – he'll never forgive you'. At the end, the pupil has to decide which advice he or she will take and say why. This may differ from the choice made in the original event.

See also: Discussion groups.

Zebra

Useful for: helping pupils realise that there are different types of questions and not all are easy to answer. Religions often address these difficult questions of value and belief.

This is a board-based variation of the 'Yes or No' activity opposite.

- You will need for each group a piece of grey sugar paper or card. On the left hand side of this is stuck a white vertical band and on the right hand side a black vertical band. In between there is a grey area – the background sheet.

- Sit pupils in groups of three or four around the 'board'. Give them a set of ten to fifteen cards prepared in advance, with statements on them which require the answers Yes or No, True or False: for example, 'Guru Nanak is the first Sikh Guru'.

- They have to place the correct answers on the black band and the incorrect answers on the white band.

- Each pupil takes it in turn to pick up a card and place it where they think it should go. If one of their group thinks that they have misplaced the card, they can move it when it comes to their turn, explaining why.

- On completion and when all have agreed the placings, pupils are given a second set of ten to fifteen cards. The activity is repeated but these statements need more subtle answers or require value judgements, for example: 'Going to the gurdwara is important'.

- Pupils realise that there are no clear-cut answers to these questions – and the grey area comes into play.

Variation

Mix the two types of card up and ask them to place them on the black or white bands. How long does it take them to realise there are two different types of questions here? What solutions do they offer?

Zoom lens or target board

Useful for: analysis of what matters most; values clarification; evaluation; encouraging speaking and listening skills.

This is a sorting, negotiating and prioritising activity suitable for both primary and secondary pupils.

- Draw five concentric circles, like a bullseye on a dartboard, on a large piece of paper. The central circle represents ' Most important', the second 'Very important', the third 'Important', the fourth 'Quite important', and the fifth 'Least important'. This provides a structure to help pupils evaluate, sort and rank statements.

- Provide pupils with a series of statements drawn from a story, or relating to religious beliefs, values and practices, or a moral or social issue such as violence or abortion.

- In pairs, pupils discuss each statement and place it on the board, justifying their opinion as they do so.

For example...

The Ten Commandments

Give pupils the Ten Commandments written on separate cards. They discuss each in turn and place it in an appropriate place on the target board. Pupils can only put one rule 'at the centre'. They must agree their corporate decision and give reasons for that decision. They then repeat the activity – this time from a Jewish or Christian point of view.

What matters most to Muslims?

After a unit of work on Islam the teacher provides pupils with a series of statements about Islam. Pupils place these as they think a Muslim would.

Index of strategies

Art 17, 18, 43
Artefacts 19–20
  Through the keyhole 32
  Hunger cloth 38
Banners 17
Books
  Making origami books 69
  Zig-zag book 69
Brainstorming 22
Circle time 61
Controversial statements
  Agree/disagree 16
Collage 17, 22
Craft
  Masks 44
Dance 23–24
Debate 24
Diary entry 25
Dilemma 15, 53
  Religious and moral
    dilemma 41
  Yardstick 76
Discussion activities
  Agenda setting 15
  Buzz groups 22
  Strategies for organising
    discussion groups 26–28
  Hotseat 36
  Wall of wisdom 75
  Yardstick 76
  Yes or no 76
Display 17
Drama 29
  Body sculpture 21, 31
  Freeze-frame 31
  Hotseat 36
  Mime 45
  Re-enactment 59
  Role-play 61–64
  Transporting a character 71
Drawing a picture 18
E-mail 30
Experiential 65
Food 42
Freeze-frame 31

Games 31–32
  Give us a clue 19
  Guess who or what? 66
  Trust games 71
Guided
  visualisation 33–35
Human
  barchart 36–37
Icebreakers 39
Interviews 27, 39, 62
ICT
  E-mail 30
  Freeze-frame
    (digital camera) 31
  Using sound files
    from websites 47
  Thought for the day 70
  (see also Video, Music
    and sound, News)
Jigsaw
  Jigsaw discussion 27
  Jigsaw reading 40
  Overhead projector 51
Knowledge and
  understanding
  Just a minute 32
  Mental maps 44
  Thinking hats 70
  Yes or no 76
  Zebra 77
Letter writing
  Agony aunts 15
  E-mail 30
Listening
  Active listening 43
  Stilling 60
Music and sound 46–47
Mystery 48–49
Mystery bag 20
News 40, 50, 70
Observation 50, 65
Pictures 40, 53, 55
Photographs 53
  Overhead projector 51
Poetry 54–55, 66
Puppets 51, 56

Questioning 57
  Hotseat 36
  Probing questions 57
  Question box 57
  Thinking hats 70
  Ultimate questions 72
  Visitors 74
  Wall of wisdom 75
  Yes and no 76
Ranking 58
Reflective activities
  Reflective diary 25
  Guided visualisation
    33–35, 59–61
  Rucksack 64
Role-play 61–63
Self-esteem, self-awareness
  Affirmation exercise 15
  I am 39
  Observation 50
  Learning about learning
    62–63
Senses 65–66
Speaking and listening
  Thinking hats 70
  (see also Discussion
    Activities, Drama)
Speculation
  Jesus comes to my town 71
Statement response
  Can of worms 27
  Everybody up! 30
  Evil game 32
  Human bar chart 36–37
  Ranking 58
  Select a statement 73
  Personal statement 73
  Yo-yo 76
Starter activities
  Affirmation exercise 15
  Natural objects 20
  Gift for life 33
Stilling 43, 59–61
Story 68
  Box story 21
  Freeze-frame 31
  Guided visualisation 33–35
  Jigsaw reading 40
  Masks 44

Mime 45
Sounds 47
Overhead projector 51
Puppets 56
Re-enactment 59
Role-play 61–63
  Making origami book 69
Thought for the day 70
Thinking skills strategies
  Mental maps 44
  Mysteries 48–49
  Community of enquiry 57
  Similarities and
    differences 67
  Thinking hats 70
Trust games 71
Ultimate questions 72
Values clarification
  Balloon debate 21
  Gift for life 33
  Values chain 52
  Rucksack 64
  Select a statement 73
  Values auction 73
  Yardstick 76
Video 24, 57
Visitors 74
  Hotseat 36
Wall of wisdom 75
Writing
  Letter writing 15
  Diary entry 25
  Diary of Reflection 25
Worship
  Hindu shrine 18
  Shabbat 18
  Sikh food 42
  Sikh music 47
  Christian music 46
  Christian places
    of worship 67
Wonder
  Moebius strip 19
  Natural objects 20

Index of themes

Anger 16, 27

Beliefs in action
In the news 40

Bible 58

Christian worship
Prayer 19, 23
Holy communion 29
Music 46

Christmas (Nativity) 29
Christmas cards 53

Christian Aid 75

Conflict
Agenda setting 15

Creation 17
Natural objects 20
Box story 21
Kaleidoscope 42

Easter 21
E-mail 30
Food 42
Masks 44

Exodus 17, 29, 47

Faith stories
Box story 21
Freeze-frame 31
Guided visualisation 33
Jigsaw reading 40
Masks 44
Mime 45
Sounds 47
Overhead projector 51
Puppets 56
Re-enactment 59
Role-play 61–63

Fear 52

Forgiveness and
reconciliation
17, 27, 37, 64

Founders of faiths
40, 57, 71

Freedom 17, 22

God 23, 46, 54, 57

Good and evil 17, 22
Evil game 32
Ramayana 51
Probing questions 57
Similarities and
differences 67
(See also Temptation)

Hanukkah 21

Heaven 27, 66

Hindu dance 24

Hindu worship 18

Hindu story 21, 29
Freeze-frame 31
Overhead projector 51
Community of
enquiry 57

Holy books
Mental maps 44
Ranking 58

Holy communion
or Eucharist 29

Home 31

Hope 17, 27, 52, 66

Human being 17

Jesus
Baptism guided
visualisation 35
Christ acrostic 54
Thinking hats 70
Transporting a character 71

Justice and injustice
Collage continuum 22

Life and death 41

Lord's prayer 23

Love 54

Marriage
Beliefs about 28

Miracles
Thinking hats 70
X Files 75

Muslim call to prayer 47

Order and pattern
Pattern in nature 20
Kaleidoscope 42

Parable
Prodigal son 25
Freeze-frame 31
Conscience corridor 76

Prayer 19
Living prayer beads 23
Paper chain 52

Peace and war
Collage continuum 22

Pentecost 17, 23

Pesach (Passover)
Music 47

Places of worship 67

Prejudice and
discrimination
Analysing a problem 16

Religious and moral
dilemma 41, 53, 76

Rites of passage 48–49

Role-play for GCSE
students
You are the examiner 63

Rules for living 28, 52, 77

Sermon on the mount 38

Sikh worship
Food 42
Music 47

Sikh khalsa
Lion cinquain 54
Mystery 48–49

Shabbat 19, 24, 29

Temptation 56
Conscience corridor 76

Ten Commandments 77

Trust 71

Violence
Agree/disagree 16

Wise words 37

Writing my
own report 63

Zacchaeus
Mime 45

Some useful resources

Learning strategies

Accelerated Learning In Practice, Alistair Smith, Network Educational Press Ltd, 2000, ISBN 1-85539-048-5

Effective Learning Activities, Chris Dickinson, Network Educational Press Ltd, 1996, ISBN 1-85539-035-3

From Thinking Skills To Thinking Classrooms, Carol Mcguinness, DfEE Research Report Rr115 (a review of approaches to developing pupils' thinking)

Six Thinking Hats, Edward De Bono, Penguin Books, ISBN 0140296662 (CD version for schools available from www.edwdebono.com/debono/shcd1.htm)

The Teacher's Toolkit, Paul Ginnis, Crown House Publishing Limited, 2002, ISBN 1-899-83-676-4

Thinking Skills And Early Childhood Education, Patrick Costello and David Fulton, 2000, ISBN 1-85345-551-8

Thinking Through Religious Education, Vivienne Baumfield and Chris Kington, 2002, ISBN 1-899857-46-X

Practical strategies for Religious Education

Building E-Bridges, Julia Ipgrave, RE Today Services, 2003, ISBN 1-904024-54-8

Decisions And Dilemmas, ed. Lat Blaylock, RE Today Services.

Picturing Jesus pack A (ISBN 1-85100-142-5, 2001) and pack B (ISBN 1-904024-44-0, 2004), Lat Blaylock, RE Today Services

Looking Inwards – Looking Outwards Student Resource Book (ISBN 1-85100-100-X) and Teacher Handbook (ISBN 1-85100-101-8), RE Today Services.

Don't Just Do Something, Sit There, Mary Stone, RMEP, 1995, ISBN 1-85175-105-X

Rethinking, Margaret Cooling with Ruth Bessant and Charlotte Key, Stapleford Centre, ISBN 1-902234-27-8

Reflections, ed. Rosemary Rivett, RE Today Services, ISBN 1–904024–07–6.

Developing RE series, RE Today Services (practical application of learning strategies to key RE themes):

Secondary *Evil and Goodness*, ed. Joyce Mackley, 2002
Codes for Living, ed. Joyce Mackley, 2002
Jesus, ed. Rosemary Rivett, 2003
Life, Death and Beyond, ed. Rosemary Rivett, 2003
Science And Religion, ed. Rosemary Rivett, 2003
Faiths in Britain Today, ed. Rosemary Rivett, 2004
Questions About God, ed. Rosemary Rivett, 2004

Primary *Special Places*, ed. Marianne Heathcote Woodbridge, 2002
Jesus, ed. Pamela Draycott, 2002
Faith Stories, ed. Joyce Mackley, 2003
Home and Family, ed. Joyce Mackley, 2003
Christmas, ed. Joyce Mackley, 2003
Words of Wisdom, ed. Joyce Mackley, 2004
Symbols of Faith, ed. Joyce Mackley, 2004
Special Times, ed. Joyce Mackley, 2004